Import Export

Importing From China
Easily and Successfully

"How I Imported for $3 and sold for $25 –
Discover my sources and exactly how to do
it!"

Mai Cheng

Exclusive Free Offer

Join other Import / Export entrepreneurs in our unique **FREE** club –

Exclusive to owners of this book. See page 28 on how to join easily in seconds (and FREE)

Connect with others members to share knowledge and experience, ask questions, discover suppliers and make contacts.

Exclusive Free Offer

Foreword

Here's how you can discover the fantastic profit margins that can be achieved by importing from China.

I've had amazing success importing thousands of products from the very small to the very large and I'd like to share with you the detailed blueprint I have used to make it both successful and profitable.

Here are my insider secrets, the exact methods I used and where I found my suppliers. By the time you have read this book you should be on your way to copying the formula.

Here's some of what I have done

Example 1 – I imported a product for under $3 and sold them for $25 (about 700% mark up!)

Example 2 – I imported another product for $85 and sold it for over $200

Example 3 – Another product cost $15 and sold for $40+

Example 4 – I have giving away a product to my valued customers that cost me $2 each but had a retail value of $15

– Use amazing offers like these to gain extra customers. I can show you how…

I'll show you the places I use to source these products and more.

Exclusive Free Offer

In fact at the moment I am working on my own product that I plan to give to Amazon to store and deliver for me.

The plan is to spend a few hours creating and sourcing the product. Then for the next few years it can earn me a nice passive income.

All I need to do is reorder from China when stocks run low. Amazon will sell and dispatch it to its worldwide customers. I won't need to do anything else!

It's still about a month away as there is a 30 day lead time before the product is sent to me but it looks very promising. Whilst not as profitable as some items the breakdown looks like this

Product Cost - $2.60
Delivery Fees (from China to here) - $0.68
Total Cost Per Product - $3.38

Currently on Amazon similar products are selling for $19.40

This gives me a difference of $16.02 but even by the time I take off Amazon fees and shipping I should make about $10 per item sold – which is ok for a few hours sourcing the product.

It has taken about 8hrs of my time over the past 3 weeks to get to this point (just going back and forward with questions, designs, changes) and $30 for the logo. I have never been to China or even spoken with these people. It's all been done by email (and no I don't speak Chinese).

I expect to sell several thousand around the world each year just using Amazon. But remember after importing the product and giving it to Amazon I have to do very little else to do to earn a passive income.

This is an amazing opportunity. I know how to sell successfully online. You may like to see my guide at http://www.CopyTheFormula.com

Knowing some of the tips that I will share with you after years of experience can save you a fortune. In fact as I write this book my office is inside one of the most successful freight forwarding companies in the country.

I know the insiders tips. You don't always have to import in large quantities. Using my methods often you can order in small numbers even when they originally quote a much higher figure.

Most of the world's huge retail companies source from China and so can the little guy.

This book is designed for you –

Here's how you can compete with Amazon, Ebay and other stores and make great margins (plus how to stop competitors eroding your margins).

Exclusive Free Offer

Discover the opportunity for yourself and use the same places some of the world's largest company's use and enjoy fantastic profit margins.

But be aware importing from China is not without risk. I cannot guarantee your success. All I can do is offer advice based on my experience.

I'd like to tell you that this is the absolute definitive book on importing from China, but the truth of the matter is that book hasn't been written yet. That book is an impossibility.

If you take 12 people and turn them loose with the same amount of money and the same list of contacts, every one of them will bring a different strategy and a different approach to importing.

What I have done here is to assemble the best basic knowledge from my notes I can compile. This is the book I wish I had read before I started attempting to define a niche and pick a product.

This is not so much a "how to" book as a "why do that" kind of book. Importing is a business where questions are as important as answers. Let me give you an example.

One of the first books I read on importing tells a story about harmonized codes, which are used to determine the amount of duty you pay on imported goods.

Exclusive Free Offer

The guy was importing wax to make candles and paying no duty at all. However, if he imported candles, he paid a 70% duty. It finally occurred to him to ask customs, "What is your definition of a candle?"

He was told that a "candle" under the harmonized codes, is wax with a wick in it. He then got customs to confirm for him via a "binding letter" that a candle with no wick was classified as "wax."

Binding letters are essentially rulings for life on how an item is classed. A copy of the letter is included in each shipment to ensure that duties are applied evenly and are not subject to interpretation.

From that time forward, he shipped in his candles pre-drilled to take a wick. His workers quickly assembled the candles once they were in the United States. He paid no duty on the candles, saving $14,000 per container!

This is the story of a brilliant importer who, because he understood a basic concept of the business, was able to apply an intuitive and unique spin and completely undercut his competition.

The basic concepts can be taught in a book. The business savvy has to be acquired "in the field" and fueled with equal parts of that magic elixir inspiration plus perspiration.

My purpose here is to offer to you the most solid introduction to basic importing concepts I can assemble. If you are an entrepreneur and willing to take that information and apply your best business instincts, you can make good money importing and have a lot of fun doing it.

If you are someone who expects every deal to go off exactly the same way every time, and if you are someone who cannot flexibly respond to the inevitable "monkey wrench" thrown into the works, importing may not be for you. For that reason, let's move on to Chapter 1 and look at the most fundamental question you will ask yourself. "Why consider importing?"

Table of Contents

Exclusive Free Offer 3

Table of Contents 10

Chapter 1 - Why Consider Importing? 17

A Real World Example.. 22

Other Advantages to Importing....................................... 22

Assess Your Personal Risk Tolerance........................... 24

.... 25

The Importance of Planning 25

Beware Complacency 26

Importing Isn't Passive Income.. 27

Exclusive Free Offer – How to Join 28

Chapter 2 – History and Philosophy in China..................... 29

China Import   P a g e | 10

Table of Contents

Historical Influences in Chinese Culture.......................... 30

The Silk Road 31

Philosophical Considerations................................... 32

The Influence of Confucius................................... 33

The Tactics of Sun Tzu...................................... 34

Chapter 3 - Researching Your Product Niche..................... 36

Avoid the Lure of Knock-Offs............................... 37

Evaluating Life Expectancy 39

Always Get Samples 39

Selecting a Product... 40

Avoid Large, Heavy Items................................... 40

Go as Simple as Possible 41

Maintain a Limited Price Range............................ 41

Don't Look for Seasonal Profit 42

Think Consumable.. 43

Thoughts on Specific Markets 44

Identifying a Target Market................................. 46

Chapter 4 – Formulating Your Business Plan 48

What is a Business Plan? 48

The Elements of a Business Plan........................... 49

Table of Contents

Executive Summary 50

Business Description 50

Marketing Strategies 50

Competition 51

Product Design and Development 52

Operations and Management 53

Financing 54

Revisit Your Plan Often 54

Chapter 5 – Locating Suppliers in China 56

Adopting the Right Mindset 56

A Fair Deal May Trump a Good Deal 57

You May Not Be Getting the Final Word 57

Always Shop Around 58

Don't Fall for Yes Men 58

Negotiable Minimum Orders 59

A Lot Can Get Lost in Translation 59

Pay Close Attention to Initial Inquiries 60

Online Supplier Portals 60

Begin with Alibaba 61

Background on Alibaba 63

Table of Contents

Global Sources 64

Contract Manufacturers and Global Sourcing 65

Chapter 6 – Traveling to China 67

Coping with Unbelievable Pollution 67

Viable Countermeasures 68

Constant Surveillance 69

Technological Monitoring 70

Physical Monitoring 71

The Issue of Language 73

Deductive vs. Inductive Communication 74

The Importance of Context 75

Humor Gone Wrong 76

Hire Translators and Interpreters 77

The Concept of Guanxi 77

"Network of Relations" 78

Refining and Maintaining Guanxi 78

Ceremonial Etiquette 80

Important Points to Remember 82

Chinese Culture and Women 83

Touring Factories 84

Table of Contents

Monitoring Factory Performance...................................... 87

Factory Audits 88

Chapter 7 – Let's Get Started...................................... 90

What You Should Have Done Already.......................... 91

Consider an Import Consultant 93

The Consultant's Role.. 94

Ownership of the Work Product............................... 95

Scope of the Consulting Activities............................ 95

Pros and Cons of Consultants 95

Matters of Compliance 96

Creating Your Brand.. 97

Product Identity 98

Logos and Packaging.. 99

Selling Your Products Online 100

Your Own Site.. 101

eBay 102

Rakuten... 105

Amazon 106

iOffer 109

Managing Barcodes.. 110

Table of Contents

Advantages of Sales Portals.. 110

Price Control 110

Cost Control 111

Targeted Product Expansion 111

Monitor Changing Margins 112

Anticipate Holiday Spikes 112

Chapter 8 – Shipping Options from China.......................... 115

What are Incoterms? 116

EXW (Ex Works).. 117

FOB (Free on Board) 117

CFR / CIF 117

Understanding Duties 117

Customs Brokers 119

Summary Thoughts on Shipping...................................... 119

Chapter 9 - Legal Considerations 121

U.S. Customs: Informal vs. Formal Entry....................... 121

Informal Entry Preferred.. 122

U.S. Tariffs and Ruling Letters 122

Protecting Your Brand Online... 123

U.S. State Sales Tax 124

Table of Contents

UK Importing Regulations 124

Afterword 127

Relevant Websites 131

Frequently Asked Questions 133

Glossary of Importing Terms 138

Index ....**Error! Bookmark not defined.**

REMEMBER 145

Exclusive Free Offer – How to Join 145

Chapter 1 - Why Consider Importing?

The clearest reason to consider importing products from China or outsourcing the production of your products to factories located in China is the oldest motivation of them all -- profit!

Either case is a win/win scenario. Small importers can match low cost but desirable products to ready markets with large profit margins, often tripling their investment. Manufacturers save huge amounts on their production costs by outsourcing, even with the cost of freight rolled in.

There are, however, many other attractive reasons to do business in the China marketplace:

Chapter 1 - Why Consider Importing?

Thriving Production Climate

About 35% to 40% of the world's production is already located in China. This fact represents tremendous cost savings to importers looking for products to bring to market, or for manufacturers seeking alternative production options for their own product lines.

Many of the factories in China are specifically designed for quick adaptation and alteration to multiple product types. They can retool quickly to respond to the needs of a new client.

This means Western businesses find a ready pool of suppliers eager to work with them and to fill their precise specifications in large quantities.

Low Cost of Labor and Production

The average savings to a company that outsources its manufacturing or sub-assembly to a vendor in China is 40% to 60% of the domestic cost.

This is due in part to the phenomenal work ethic in China, which drives laborers seeking to escape rural poverty to work almost inhuman hours voluntarily.

There are also fewer standard "rules" in China. The lack of consistent regulation is a double-edged sword that can open the door for exploitive treatment of laborers, but also allow for a flexible business climate in which costs can be held to a minimum.

Chapter 1 - Why Consider Importing?

Hands of Regulatory Environment

China is still young as an industrialized nation. Its laws and regulations are more subject to local interpretation. This can work for or against Western businessmen, but in general the Chinese government at all levels takes a hands-off approach to business.

This is not to say that in your dealings in China you do not have a moral obligation to ensure that your products are being made in factories where workers are treated well and that safety standards are met.

Perhaps you recall the furor that surrounded Kathie Lee Gifford's line of clothing sold in Walmart stores. It was revealed that 12-year-old laborers in Bangladesh were sewing the items; a fact that outraged human rights activists around the globe and created a public relations nightmare for Gifford and her products.

These kinds of scenarios should be avoided at all costs, both on an ethical level, and on a PR one, but that being said, there are still advantages to be exploited legitimately in a business climate with less government oversight than that present in most Western nations.

China Grows as an Export Market

China isn't just a source for importing items for sale elsewhere in the world. The country is the fastest growing export market for American goods and services thanks to an expanding Chinese middle class hungry for goods from the West.

The more Westernized China becomes in its tastes, the more facile the business climate will become as well. There are certainly complex cultural waters to be negotiated, a factor I will discuss at length, but in general understanding is growing on both sides of the business equation.

This will, over time, make business dealings less subject to the kinds of cultural hurdles that now must be overcome.

My Approach in Writing This Book

There are many "how to" books on importing from China, and many layers of the import business itself. You may simply be someone who wants to work from home and import a few items for sale online.

I have done this. For several years I imported earrings from China that I then sold online with excellent margins. As with any online endeavor, however, I had to also fight site rankings to get my products noticed, an issue Google in particular has made very hard for Internet marketers.

I have also sold some of my own branded items, primarily jigsaw puzzles, which I outsourced for manufacture in China. These also sold well, and introduced me to the complexities of the Chinese business culture, which I will discuss in this book.

Chapter 1 - Why Consider Importing?

I will try to address importing broadly so that the information can be scaled up or down according to your individual business goals.

Make no mistake, regardless of the level at which you are dealing with Chinese suppliers, you will have less success and lower profits if you don't cultivate this understanding.

This aspect of the necessary "know how" is in addition to the nuts and bolts "how to" items that form the *process* rather than the *philosophy* of importing.

The "trick," if you want to call it that, in selecting any importing niche is to purchase well below the market price and then sell to a middleman or directly to customers for an amount at or near the going rate.

I prefer to think of this as a skill rather than a trick because anyone can learn to do just that kind of buying and selling.

Chapter 1 - Why Consider Importing?

Let's start with a specific example to illustrate what kinds of margins you'll be attempting to create.

A Real World Example

Let's consider a product for which there seems to be an evergreen niche in the world of apparel -- jeans. If you shop at a retail store, you will pay at least $40 for a brand of jeans that are considered to be stylish.

The store has purchased that clothing from a supplier and marked the price up to turn a profit. Chances are good the supplier acquired the product for around $20, with the store marking them up 50%.

But where did the supplier get the jeans? If they're smart, they imported them from China and paid about $2 each, making an $18 profit per pair.

Of course, that's not assuming expenses, but I think you can see where this is headed. If you know *what* to import, *how* to import it, and *where* to sell what you import, you can make money.

Other Advantages to Importing

There are many other advantages to getting into the import business. Much of the work can now be accomplished in online marketplaces like Alibaba, which I'll discuss later in this book, but importing still creates the opportunity to travel.

Chapter 1 - Why Consider Importing?

If you want to go overseas to do your buying, and the idea of immersing yourself in a foreign business culture is appealing, importing can be a fascinating experience for those reasons alone.

Here's a good example of the difference in business etiquette. In China, business cards are always exchanged upon meeting someone and are presented with both hands as a sign of respect.

The card should be translated into the simplified Chinese characters used on the mainland. Failure to supply a translated card can be seen as offensive and may well doom a potential business relationship before any negotiating can even begin.

We'll talk more about the etiquette of doing business in China, but this simple example shows you that if you are intrigued by the art of business and dealing, China will be a whole new world for you. In the beginning, you won't be able to "speak the language" in more ways than one.

The China marketplace poses unique challenges to a businessperson's skill set, requiring a completely different approach to negotiation and deal making. For many skilled importers, however, this is a large part of the interest in this type of business model.

In the beginning, no matter how many books you've read or experts you've consulted, you will feel overwhelmed. No one who has started an importing business has done so flawlessly and without making mistakes.

The Chinese culture can be endlessly confusing and the logistics of traveling to China thoroughly intimidating. Thankfully, there are ways to mitigate these effects. Fear of these factors should not keep you from pursuing importing as a way to earn a living.

It is absolutely possible to import from China, right from your living room. For many, this is the real attractiveness of running this kind of business.

Importing has been transformed by the Internet. It is not only possible but also completely practical to run your import business from your laptop anywhere in the world you want to be.

Assess Your Personal Risk Tolerance

A word of warning. If you are not comfortable with some degree of risk in your business dealings, then being an importer is not for you.

Risk is inherent in business. In the import business, you will run the risk of making decisions that will not produce the result you had hoped for.

You might select the niche/wrong product, or misjudge the market and get stuck with loads of inventory. This is where detailed research is vital.

If you are a businessperson -- a real entrepreneur at heart -- you already understand that no matter how carefully you work out your business plan; it is impossible to remove all risk from any endeavor.

If the China import business model appeals to you, and you take the time to study the methods that ensure reasonable success, there are compelling reasons to move forward with this business.

Anyone who has ever started an import business has picked a "dud" product at least once. Most importers, however, get better and better at the game the longer they play it.

The Importance of Planning

The most important step in creating an import business is to form a business plan in advance. This involves all the following steps *at minimum*:

- Research a product niche to determine your primary market.

- Research products within that niche, including an assessment of their life expectancy in terms of buyer demand.

- Identify your target market and assess the degree to which it is saturated by the competition.

- Pick your product and locate potential suppliers.

- Locate potential resellers.

- Run a full cost analysis of your start-up expenses and reconcile those amounts with your available financing.

- If necessary, determine the level of investment required and seek financing.

- Estimate your earning potential and prepare a prospectus and other necessary materials to secure financing.

In the following chapters, I'll discuss these major points and try to give you as much insight as I can to start out as an importer. Let me be clear, however, that you'll never stop learning this business.

Beware Complacency

Complacency in any kind of business is never a good thing, but in importing it's particularly serious. Suppliers come and go. Products slip in and out of popularity. Laws change.

Chapter 1 - Why Consider Importing?

You never just learn the import business once. To stay on top of your game, be prepared to constantly re-examine and adjust what you're doing.

For some readers that immediately raises an exciting business challenge, while others have already started to cringe and back away.

Only you can decide if this is an arena in which you'll feel comfortable competing. You definitely need to continue educating yourself and keep up with what's going on in this industry.

Importing Isn't Passive Income

There's been a lot of talk in recent years about "passive income," which basically is the ability to make money while you sleep. There isn't a person alive who isn't interested in finding a way to do that very thing. However, the business of importing is not about generating passive income.

I bring this up in the beginning because there are many people who see importing as a way to make lots of money without doing much work. While there are many businesses that create passive income for an entrepreneur, a successful import business is not one of them.

This is a business in which you will have to be actively involved. If you're not prepared to do that, don't throw your money away or waste your time.

Exclusive Free Offer – How to Join

Join other entrepreneurs in our unique **FREE** club –

It's quick and easy to sign up. Connect with others members to share knowledge and experience, ask questions, discover suppliers and make contacts

Here's how in 2 simple steps…

Step 1

Go to http://www.ImportingExpert.com
Enter your name and email address and click 'Join.'

Step 2

Confirm your subscription. As soon as you sign up, we'll send you an email asking you to confirm the details are correct. Just click the link in the email and you'll be joined free.

If you don't receive the email, please check your spam folder and that you used the correct email address.

It's as easy as that.

Chapter 2 – History and Philosophy in China

Both America and the United Kingdom are nations with rich business histories. The industrial revolution in the UK not only gave birth to modernized methods of manufacturing, but also comprised a vast social revolution for the British people.

In the United States, the captains of industry who dominated the Gilded Age carved out great legacies for themselves in the business history of the nation.

While the likes of John D. Rockefeller might not be an ethical example of how to build a company, Standard Oil was still an impressive achievement, as was the Ford Motor Company under the direction of the dour and parsimonious Henry Ford.

And you don't need to understand ANY of that to be a successful businessperson in either Britain or America! In China, however, history underlies everything. History infuses the public consciousness and affects all aspects of commerce on a day-to-day basis.

Historical Influences in Chinese Culture

An imperial government ruled China for more than 3,000 years. For the last 500 of those years, the Emperor was ensconced in the Forbidden City, a rigidly walled enclave in which no commerce was allowed.

This imperial isolation created a system in which the provinces were ruled by local governments that in turn reported to the imperial government. This diffused hierarchy did not fundamentally change under Communist rule.

Westerners expect that laws and regulations will be formulated by a central source, which they take to be Beijing. It's difficult at first to understand that these laws and regulations, once promulgated, are highly subject to interpretation at all local levels.

The Western mind is accustomed to a system in which laws are passed at the national level and interpreted not by officials, but by the court systems. This vast body of interpretative law overlays and enriches our legislation.

You must balance a perception of this radically different legal climate with the fact that trading and business are an integral part of the Chinese psyche. The Western world as we know it today was deeply influenced by early trade from China.

The Silk Road

The collection of trade routes that stretched between Europe and the Orient during the Middle Ages and the beginning of the Renaissance were collective known as the Silk Road.

These routes not only carried trade goods, but cultural and technological ideas that fundamentally changed the Western world and brought China out of her self-imposed isolation and into contact with radically different cultures.

The ports of Hong Kong and Shanghai became central to the infrastructure of trade in China and remain so today. Unfortunately, some of the merchants, referred to as "water people" in Chinese history texts, dealt in items that were highly prized commodities like tea and opium.

While I am not interested in writing a history of China, it's important to understand that this situation allowed the Christian religion to make evangelical inroads into China, and for the British to seize control of Hong Kong for more than 100 years.

We are talking about events that took place in the 1840s, but to this day, religious evangelists are only barely tolerated in

China and then only if they obey the law and maintain an extremely low profile.

There are lessons in this situation for Western business people as well. The period from 1850 to 1949 is referred to in China as the Hundred Years of Humiliation.

It was a time when European and Japanese traders were in control of Chinese seaports, and unwelcome religious ideas were foisted on the Chinese people.

These feelings of occupation and subjugation were made much worse by the Japanese occupation of China during World War II.

Although the modern Chinese are perfectly willing to do business with the West, there is a cultural memory of resentment toward foreigners.

In almost all instances, the laws require that the ownership in any enterprise involving foreigners place the Chinese stockholders in the majority.

The Communist years brought additional levels of suffering in an effort to reclaim the industrial life of the nation, and laid down a new layer of socialist suspicion aimed against Western capitalists.

Philosophical Considerations

Interwoven in all these complex political threads are crosscurrents of essential philosophy very alien to the

Western mind. These include the teachings of Confucius and Sun Tzu.

The Influence of Confucius

The teachings of Confucius are so fundamental to the Chinese way of life that his principles are taught in the nation's elementary schools.

Confucius, who lived from 551-479 BCE, was a political figure and philosopher educator who founded the Ru School of Chinese Thought, emphasizing the values of:

- study
- restraint
- respect
- consideration

These qualities are the hallmarks of the national culture.

These values not only influence how individuals lead their own lives, but how they interact with one another in conversation and in business negotiation.

The concept of saving face is pervasive. Your Chinese hosts will never disagree with you in public. You will likely encounter a situation in which your every instruction is greeted with smiling, nodding, agreement and assent. Even if no one in the room agrees with you in the slightest!

You must gain the trust of your hosts. Draw them out with appropriately framed questions in order to discover their true ideas about the topic at hand. If you don't, you may not find out for months that serious disagreements do indeed exist and are affecting your business operations.

The Tactics of Sun Tzu

While *The Art of War* by Sun Tzu is a military treatise dating from the 6th century BC, many businesspeople in China negotiate with tactics drawn directly from this text.

For instance, if you visit China to discuss a potential business partnership, your hosts will mention the details of your return flight, indicating that everything will be taken care of by that date.

They will then take you out to dinner and a round of sightseeing before excusing themselves to attend an unexpected meeting. You won't hear from your host again until shortly before your scheduled departure.

The reasoning behind this behavior is that if you are in a rush to catch your plane, you'll be more likely to accept their terms than risk missing your flight by taking the time to negotiate.

Sun Tzu counseled his readers to pick their own time and place to fight, which is precisely what your host is attempting to do in delaying the negotiations until you are at a perceived disadvantage in regard to time.

I'm certainly not an expert on the text of *The Art of War*, but I can tell you that there are many versions of the book with very useful commentaries that can give insight into standard tactics of business negotiation, which you will encounter.

Many are written specifically for business people including:

- Mark R. McNeilly, *Sun Tzu and the Art of Business: Six Strategic Principles for Managers*

- Gerald A. Michaelson and Steven Michaelson, *Sun Tzu - The Art of War for Managers: 50 Strategic Rules Updated for Today's Business*.

Chapter 3 - Researching Your Product Niche

If I were talking from the perspective of an Internet marketer about researching a niche, this would be the portion of the book that discusses using this or that keyword tool to determine what people are searching for online.

I'd be instructing you on how to find a broad area of interest into which you would "drill down" to arrive at a set of keywords to which an arcane set of numbers are placed.

After learning what amounts to a degree in the "physics" of Internet math, you'd pick a set of keywords and roll the dice. You could match them up with content and product or service offerings that would – in time -- generate a profit.

Then, after all that, Google would change its algorithm, invalidate all your work, force you to start your research over, and likely rethink your entire marketing strategy!

That's why we're not talking about Internet marketing!

When you import products from China for resale in your chosen country and do it properly, that kind of uncertainty is largely eliminated from the work.

That is not to say that importing from China doesn't carry its own fair share of risks, but you do stand a better chance of learning the ropes and working the process intelligently.

Avoid the Lure of Knock-Offs

The luxury accessory and apparel niche is one to which most new Internet marketers gravitate. There are always buyers for counterfeit copies of any big name designer item.

However, it's entirely possible – and in fact likely – that the people who own the trademark on those products will ultimately shut you down.

If you try to sell knock-offs, you may make a little money, but you won't be building a business. You'll be running a scheme.

I'm an entrepreneur. I didn't get into this just for the money, and I certainly didn't get into it to deal with potential legal hassles.

Don't get me wrong, I want the money, but I also want a business that reflects my own hard work, good judgment, and understanding of the marketplace.

In other words, I want to be able to be proud of my business, grow it intelligently, and not have to talk in hushed tones about my questionable sources for knock-off Prada bags!

Chapter 3 - Researching Your Product Niche

Evaluating Life Expectancy

When you hear people talk about the life expectancy of a product, they are really talking about the potential for long-term demand. Using the Internet marketing example, the ideal products are those that are "evergreen."

These are the things that sold well in 1975 and are still selling well in 2014 in the same or a highly similar form. Those products are not easy to find, but when you have one, it's golden.

There's always money to be made in fads – for a SHORT time. Think about things like mood rings or pet rocks. For a very brief period of time, people just HAD to have them, and then the fad was over (although I do see mood rings making a comeback.)

There are no magic formulas for evaluating life expectancy, and the more you work in the import market, you'll get a better feel for this process. I'm not saying to always avoid the "faddish" products, but don't let them form the foundation of your business.

Always Get Samples

This is a point I'm likely to make over and over again. Always, always, always get samples of products before you order in bulk.

Some suppliers make it difficult and more expensive to order small amounts, but wouldn't you rather get stuck with 25 widgets you can't sell as opposed to 2,500? Even if the sample does cost more, you'll save money, time, and effort in the long run.

No product that is shoddily made will sell well, and it certainly won't garner repeat business. Samples also allow you to conduct market tests, so those 25 widgets may be worth more than you initially imagine. Consider it one of the many costs of doing business.

Selecting a Product

You'll find tons of advice about selecting your products, and as you become more experienced, you'll develop the "wisdom" that works for you. In the beginning, however, I think you'll be much more successful if you adhere to the following guidelines.

Avoid Large, Heavy Items

Dealing with shipping large, heavy items to the States or anywhere else in the world for that matter is a huge headache, and will rapidly eat into your potential profits.

Keep your product — especially your first product — small and light so your shipping costs are low and your profit margin is high.

Go as Simple as Possible

I'm personally a big fan of "easy" any way, but you definitely want an easy product. By that, I mean one that is simple to make in terms of process.

The lower the potential for production error, the fewer moving parts, the more direct the purpose and use, the less headache for you.

With technically complex products, you also run the risk that the item will not conform to specifications used in Western countries and that it cannot be reliably reproduced in large quantities.

Maintain a Limited Price Range

Everyone brings differing amounts of start-up capital to the import business, but I suggest that you keep the cost of your first product as low budget as possible, like $10-$150.

This is the same logic that applies to the idea of keeping it simple. Expensive items are expensive to ship. You'll also have less margin for error in quality control, and probably a harder time finding a reliable target market.

I tried to avoid the word "cheap" in the section header. You want products that are inexpensively made, not cheap, but are good quality and with ready demand.

Don't Look for Seasonal Profit

We've all said things like, "Man! I'll bet that business makes a killing at Christmas!" Well, that's great, but what do they do the other 11 months of the year? Do you really want to base your whole business on one month of sales?

For the most part, you want to find items that will sell year round. If you concentrate on a seasonal item, you'll be storing plastic snowmen in your garage and they won't be paying you any rent!

I am not suggesting you completely ignore the potential for seasonal profit, but rather that you do not count on such limited sales as the whole foundation for your business.

If you do go with a seasonal product, make sure it's one that has year-over-year longevity so you can move leftover inventory in the next sales cycle.

Think Consumable

When you pick items that are consumable, you have the potential for long-term, repeat customers. Too many people hear the word "consumable" and confuse it with "edible." By "consumable," I mean anything that wears out, needs replacing, or needs restocking regularly.

If, for instance, you're importing ear buds that you sell to a shop in lots of 200 or 300, the idea is that the retailer moves the product and wants to restock buying from you. So, in that sense, those ear buds are "consumable."

Concentrate on cultivating a market for your products that is built around ongoing relationships rather than one-time sales.

Thoughts on Specific Markets

Designer apparel and accessory knock-offs are popular for beginning importers due to the vast size of the market for those items. The same is true for the gift and décor market.

Good taste can work against you.

My major problem with both of these niches is the matter of taste. Having good taste can be the kiss of death!

Often it's the tackiest items that sell, and some people just can't read the market well enough to pick an item with sufficiently broad consumer appeal.

Good buyers will tell you that for the American market only about 5% to 10% of purchases are "good taste." Now, of course, taste is a matter of personal perception, but let's put it this way:

You'll sell more religious scenes on black velvet than reproductions of a French impressionist painting -- even though poor Monet is rolling in his grave over the number of mouse pads stamped with his beautiful water lilies.

My point is simply that judging what people will buy in either of these areas takes a practiced eye.

Specialized knowledge may or may not help.

Sometimes having specialized knowledge of a profession or hobby can be a big plus – if you are current with the subject. Let's use an example that could fit either category, photography.

I knew a beginning importer who had worked as a wedding photographer before taking a desk job for a number of years.

As retirement age was coming on, he decided to start looking into importing items from China for sale on eBay and in the "real world."

He knew, from his past experience, that photographers use a lot of clear plastic sleeves to hold proofs and finished prints as a means of protecting the surface.

The man located a supplier of plastic sleeves in standard photo print sizes and bought hundreds of thousands of them for just pennies each. He started trying to sell them online, and by contacting photo supply houses.

That's when his crucial mistake came to light. He had completely missed out on the digital photography revolution and didn't realize that most proofs today are viewed on computer screens.

In this case, the new importer was able to adjust. There are still plenty of uses for plastic sleeves in various craft industries like handmade greeting card production. Various collectors also use them to protect vintage postcards and similar items.

The "newbie" had to scramble around and do market research that he should have done in the first place. He did, ultimately, unload all of the plastic sleeves, but it took a long time. Although he technically got his money back, it's highly questionable as to whether or not he made a profit.

There are actually two lessons in that story. Do your market research and don't just jump right in because you KNOW a product will sell -- it probably won't!

Identifying a Target Market

There are many good online sources to help new importers judge potential markets, but you can start with a very simple and straightforward approach – Google Product Search at www.google.com/shopping.

Use the Google "Shortlists" to find out what people are searching for and buying online, as well as to gauge new trends that are popping up.

Another good resource is the listing of popular items on eBay at popular.ebay.com. EBay isn't just a place for used items and collectibles: it's a prime marketplace to sell items you import.

And finally, just go to Amazon and take a look at the bestsellers page found at www.amazon.com/gp/bestsellers.

Make a list of the top selling 10-20 products on each site and find the ones that appear in all three places. These are good leads to begin focused searching for overseas suppliers on portal sites like Alibaba.

While this is hardly a "scientific" approach, it will get you thinking in terms of supply and demand, which is key to the whole import model.

Chapter 4 – Formulating Your Business Plan

If you're even thinking about skipping this chapter, stop right now. This is NOT an optional part of becoming an importer.

For one thing, if you have to seek financing for your import business, you'll need to have a formally drawn up business plan.

That's not the "how to" book I'm writing, but if you don't know how to formulate such a plan, you need to learn -- or you need to hire a consultant to help you.

Once you have decided on a product to import begin creating your business plan. Whether you have your financing already in place or not, you need a business plan for YOU!

What is a Business Plan?

A well-conceived business plan will include the answers to the following questions:

- What are the goals of my business?
- What are my business strategies?
- What are the potential problems I will face?
- What is the organizational structure of my business?
- How much money do I need to make this happen?

Everyone who begins any kind of business should ponder these points. A formal business plan will help you to move forward by first recognizing where the potential roadblocks to your success might be.

The Elements of a Business Plan

As someone who is prone to dive right in and never read the instructions, I can't emphasize enough how much I think you should draw up a written plan for your import business.

It doesn't matter if it's written in pencil on a legal pad or typed up in a word processor. Your business plan represents an important thought process that you should work through to give your import business the best start possible. Think of your business plan as that moment of stopping to take a breath before you dive in.

Executive Summary

Every business plan starts with an executive summary that describes the business or, in the case of importing, the product or products you want to acquire and sell.

If you are trying to get a loan or interest investors, the executive summary should also include the amount of the required capital.

Business Description

The executive summary should be followed by a business description. These two elements are not the same thing so don't scrimp on the description.

This section should go into greater detail about the structure of the business, the industry or market into which your product fits, and why the item is unique and therefore marketable.

Marketing Strategies

Logically then, your marketing strategies should be outlined next. In fact, I think these questions are so crucial I want to break them out as a list:

- What is your market?
- How big is the market?

- Is the market growing?
- What is the sale potential for your product?
- Can you target a specific market share?
- How will you set your pricing structure?
- What are the channels and costs of distribution?
- How will you market to wholesalers?

These are the questions that most new importers fail to ask before ordering from a supplier. Just forcing yourself to do all of this research is a critical argument in favor of a written business plan!

Competition

Although it may be hard to specifically identify your competitors for a product by name, you can make a real effort to look at market saturation.

For instance, if you decide you want to import screen protectors for computer tablets to sell on eBay, research all the other vendors selling the same product.

I picked this example on purpose. Screen protectors are such a "good" idea you can find literally thousands of listings. Getting your screen protectors noticed from all the others being listed would be a tough proposition.

Your products will not sell well in an over-saturated market unless there's something that really makes them stand out.

Product Design and Development

For importers, this is really more an area to discuss your supply chain and narrowing down your final product selection. Questions you might consider here include, but are not limited to:

- Where will you get the product?
- How much will it cost?
- How many do you have to buy?
- If the volume price is lower, how much can you sell?
- How much margin for error is there in the manufacture?
- Is there a market for liquidation if you get a bad batch?
- Can you get samples and conduct a market test?

Ask yourself every question you can think of about your product, and never go forward without samples and a market test! Even if you have to buy 25-50 items, bite the bullet and test with those before ordering 10 times as many that you'll never be able to move.

Operations and Management

If you are a small importer working from home, this section may not be necessary. Typically small importers don't need a "staff," but as your business grows, this could be an area you need to re-visit.

I've found it's often hard to transition a home business to a more organized mode of operation. You get used to doing things yourself. When delegation becomes necessary, you don't do it well, or you spend money on "help" that is no help at all.

At the very least, use this section of your business plan to name the major players in your line of supply. What if one of these entities goes out of business? What is your alternate source to buy or move your product?

Financing

Describing your financing is also not an optional step in formulating a business plan, even if you have all the money in place to get started.

Importers working alone from home are AWFUL about keeping track of this information. If you're not tracking your income, keeping your balance sheets, and tracking your cash flow, I promise, you will be losing money somewhere!

The financing section of your business plan is also a good place to get in touch with your comfort level for risk. From the beginning, you should decide what would constitute that "throw in the towel" moment.

How much money can you commit to becoming an importer? What will success look like to you? What will failure look like?

Ask these hard questions in the early stages, not when you've spent every dime you have on the project and have a garage full of widgets from China you can't give away.

Revisit Your Plan Often

A business plan is not sacred text handed down on the mountain and carved in stone. Your business goals can and should change over time.

You'll make adjustments according to successes and failures, changes in the marketplace, alterations in your supply chain – and for a million other reasons I can't even begin to list.

Revisit your business plan often, using the document as a tool to check the "blood pressure" of your business. If you've diverged significantly from your original vision, ask yourself why.

- Are the changes a natural response to the "real world" factors you've encountered?
- Do they make good business sense?
- Are you on track?
- Is there a need for a "course correction?"

Changing your business plan to reflect what's actually happening in your business is not an indicator of "success" or "failure," but it is a sign of active engagement!

As an importer, the most crucial initial step in formulating your business plan is deciding what you are going to sell.

Chapter 5 – Locating Suppliers in China

Your understanding of the Chinese and their business culture will evolve and grow over time, but the only way to really get started after you've determined your niche is to just dive in. The following section will explore key points in finding a supplier.

Adopting the Right Mindset

As I indicated earlier, finding a supplier or contracting with a manufacturer can be done in a relatively "small" way via an online source, or through on-the-ground negotiations.

At the end of this chapter I'll talk about online portals to find suppliers in China, and in the next chapter we'll assume that you plan to fly to China and conduct your negotiations in person.

There are key points to remember, however, regardless of how you contact and work with your supplier.

A Fair Deal May Trump a Good Deal

When working with sellers from China, everything is negotiable. Work for a FAIR deal for both parties. You could lose contact with a good supplier with whom you might have a long-term relationship by focusing too much on price and not enough on other beneficial aspects of the deal.

I always caution people new to importing not to engage in "penny wise, pound foolish" strategies. While it is true that you can work with suppliers from China with considerably less expense than those you will find in the West, don't lose sight of the crucial distinction between "inexpensive" and "cheap."

I firmly believe that there comes a point in every deal when trying to go "cheap," really isn't a savings. Strive to keep your expenses at the lowest level possible, but realize that everyone in a deal has to make money at some point for there to be mutual satisfaction in the arrangement.

You May Not Be Getting the Final Word

Understand that you may not actually be negotiating with the manufacturer of the item, but a middleman seller. If you are not getting clear answers to your questions, consider working with another seller, or ask if you can get more details about the manufacturing process.

This should help you to determine if you're dealing with someone who can really help you get what you need or if you only have a salesman on the line.

Always Shop Around

If you find a product with one supplier, you can bet someone else is selling it on another site or through another channel. Always compare and get several different prices and samples.

If comparison-shopping is important for any major purchase, it is even more important in locating a foreign supplier. You may find a hidden gem -- the product you want at a lower price for better terms!

Don't Fall for Yes Men

If you are inquiring about having a product made, most manufacturers will say "yes" immediately with no real consideration of what they can really do for you.

Don't take their word for it! Ask for references and samples!

Remember that the person on the other end of the exchange wants your business and may be promising things they cannot deliver.

Never establish a business relationship where money is exchanged until you have proof that the manufacturer can deliver.

Negotiable Minimum Orders

Minimum order quantity (MOQ) levels are negotiable, but you may have to pay more per unit. This is always a difficult decision point, especially for new importers.

Do you want a rock bottom price only to get stuck with 5,000 units, or are you willing to pay a little more for a smaller lot to really conduct a more valid market test?

A Lot Can Get Lost in Translation

The language barrier is real when dealing with suppliers in China and can be a major stumbling block, one to which we will come back a bit later on. For now, understand that some of the language-based misconceptions you will encounter are simple, but so crucial they cannot be ignored.

For instance, in the West when someone answers, "yes," the word implies agreement. In China, "yes" means the person to whom you are speaking has understood what you've said.

The "yes" does not, however, imply agreement or disagreement. It's completely neutral and you have to seek confirmation for agreement through further negotiations.

Also, don't assume fluency in English, in fact assume just the opposite. It is highly likely that the people with whom you are dealing – especially if the negotiations are carried out via email -- are relying on translation programs to decipher your inquiries and compose their responses. Use simple, easily understood English and be very clear about all numbers! Don't be afraid to repeat yourself, and to ask for confirmation. Make sure that you understand what the supplier has said – and that the supplier understands what he's said.

Pay Close Attention to Initial Inquiries

The initial inquiry can set the tone for the entire negotiation. Be clear and concise. Tell the supplier what you are looking for, and the quality you require. Ask for pricing details subject to negotiation and request a sample.

By the time you're talking with a supplier, you should have thoroughly researched your product. You should know such things as the going market price and the acceptable range of quality for the item.

If you are not already an expert on the product you wish to sell, you are much more likely to be scammed by a disreputable supplier.

Online Supplier Portals

The Internet is a natural venue to make your initial contacts. Of the many marketplaces for China products that you will encounter, I believe you should start with the biggest, Alibaba.

You will read a great deal about people who are scammed working on this site, but that is, in my opinion, a product of too many folks diving in to ordering and paying for products before they understand the fundamentals of importing.

Begin with Alibaba

The issue in finding suppliers in China is not availability but ubiquity – to the point of complete overload for importing "newbies."

When you are seeking to have a product made in high quantities or to purchase a ready made product, you will be faced with multiple companies that are anxious to do business with you. Finding a reliable supplier for smaller amounts is much harder.

For this reason, most new importers should at least begin with Alibaba.com since you can search manufacturers by category and even post requests for information.

When you begin to look around Alibaba you will see that member suppliers post a lot of items for sale, everything from parts to T-shirts.

These people are typically manufacturing representatives or sales companies. They may have connections at multiple factories.

Chapter 5 – Locating Suppliers in China

In dealing with these people, you are introducing another layer in the transaction, which can limit your control and increase your costs. However, the ease of access at Alibaba often mitigates these potential negatives.

In order to protect yourself while dealing with suppliers, always be very clear about your requirements. Use simple, direct terms. It's imperative that the supplier or manufacturer knows exactly what you want. Be precise about things like:

- weight
- thickness
- colors
- size
- material quality

There is no such thing as too much detail in formulating your specifications. Giving the supplier sufficient detail will prevent delays, disappointments, and misunderstandings.

Also, no matter how detailed you are, you'll still get a lot of questions, which you should answer patiently and completely.

Do not be surprised if you receive quotes for large minimum quantity orders in multiples of 1000. This may not be a deal breaker if you have done your market research and are confident you can either sell or liquidate the items.

Chapter 5 – Locating Suppliers in China

Chinese manufacturers excel at producing large quantities at low prices, so be prepared to think through this trade off as you formulate your business plans. You don't want to get stuck with excess inventory, but you do want to keep your margins high.

Background on Alibaba

The Alibaba site is located at www.alibaba.com. The company offers a comprehensive domestic and foreign trade platform for business-to-business marketing.

The Alibaba Group describes itself as "a family of Internet-based businesses with a mission to make it easy for anyone to buy or sell anywhere in the world."

Founded in 1999, the privately held company maintains more than 70 offices in China, India, Singapore, the United States, and the United Kingdom.

Alibaba is attractive to new importers because it is a "one-stop" all inclusive service, but if you begin to read reviews online, the word "scam" does get tossed around a great deal. In part, this is due to the site's huge scope.

In 2010, Alibaba CEO David Wei said in an interview that the company has 1.3 million global suppliers with another six million in China. Of those, 100,000 were verified Gold suppliers in China. The trick to finding a reputable supplier is to **only work with gold-rated members**.

Global Sources

Alibaba is not the only online marketplace for finding suppliers and manufacturers in China. You can also use Global Sources, which can be found at www.globalsources.com.

The company, which is based in Hong Kong, also facilitates trade from China, providing sourcing information to volume buyers and integrated marketing services to suppliers.

Registration for Global Sources is free for the basic services offered including product and supplier search and inquiry. Users fill out a form to inquire about products, and multiple inquiries can be sent at once via the "Inquiry Basket."

Currently about 1 million international buyers use Global Sources for product and company information, including 95 of the top 100 retailers in the world.

This is a slightly more advanced marketplace, and one you should explore after learning the ropes on Alibaba.

Contract Manufacturers and Global Sourcing

For companies and brands that don't want to own and operate factories, contract manufacturers are a good option. These entities provide engineering and manufacturing services. They are experts at adapting their operations to your products and thus achieving smooth, repeatable production lines.

Many contract manufacturers work with various aspects of electronics including:

- Hon Hai Precision Industry (Foxconn)
- Flextronics
- Jabil

Global sourcing companies are also an excellent resource as they maintain ongoing relationships with a network of qualified manufacturers. Working through a sourcing company can mitigate risks to your supply chain caused by everything from material shortages to natural disasters.

Chapter 5 – Locating Suppliers in China

Many global sourcing entities work in the areas of apparel and footwear including:

- Li & Fung
- Mast Industries

If you are interested in contract manufacturers or global sourcing companies, I recommend that you work through your first deals with an importing consultant.

If you attempt to enter importing at this level, you will need the advice and guidance of qualified professionals until you are comfortable navigating the business climate on your own.

Chapter 6 – Traveling to China

The cultural shock of your first trip to China can be overwhelming. There are so many ways in which you need to prepare yourself for the experience it's almost difficult to know where to begin – and not all of those factors are even business related!

Coping with Unbelievable Pollution

Of all the things you may try to anticipate, nothing can even begin to describe the high levels of pollution you will encounter. Even the images you've seen on television don't really give you an idea of the reality of air so thick it looks like you can slice it in pieces.

Much of the atmospheric contaminants in China come from the high levels of sulfur dioxide and nitrogen oxides pumped out by plants that still burn coal. The detectable levels are so high, the particulate matter travels as far as Los Angeles, California.

The deplorable air quality is so pervasive, you see it, smell it, and even feel it. The streets are filled with taxis emitting plumes of black diesel smoke curling skyward to join a veritable toxic mélange of chemicals.

Not only will you be negotiating a foreign business climate, you will likely be doing it feeling absolutely awful! Expect watering eyes, a burning throat, and before long, a hacking cough.

If you're looking out a window from a high-rise in Beijing, you won't be able to see the ground. Many businessmen say that in the entire time they were in the city, they never saw the sun, just a sky full of thick, brown haze.

Viable Countermeasures

As an importer, you'll be going in and out of this poisonous soup regularly. I recommend staying inside in an air-conditioned environment as much as possible, preferably one with air filtration.

For this reason, you should stay at western hotels that adhere to global performance standards. You want in-room air-conditioning. Think Marriott, Hyatt, or Hilton. Even there, you may feel the need to place a wet towel over the air conditioner to serve as additional filtration.

Sip purified bottled water all day. Don't buy it from a street vendor! Use throat lozenges as necessary. Antihistamines can also be useful, but you don't want to get too dried out. Good hydration under these conditions is extremely important.

If you wear contacts, leave them at home. The level of grime and grit that will accumulate under the lenses will only irritate your eyes and in turn make them even more susceptible to the pollution levels. Travel in hired cars, not taxis, and when you're outside wear a surgical mask.

All of these precautions are necessary not only to protect your lungs from the harmful effects of the bad air, but also to help you feel well enough to tend to your business dealings effectively.

Constant Surveillance

A reasonably healthy degree of paranoia is not out of line when you visit China. If you feel as if you are being watched, or have the sense that your movements are being tracked, you're probably correct.

It is highly likely that both your comings and goings and any work that you conduct online while you are in China will be monitored. You must understand that maintaining the status quo is the major mission of the Chinese government.

The Communist officials constantly gather information with an eye toward curbing the activities of dissidents and any others who would seek to create conflict for the state.

Technological Monitoring

Although the government cannot control the content of international websites, they can and do take measure to control the flow of information in and out of the nation and to prevent citizens from openly discussing government affairs.

Chinese websites that take the risk of displaying sensitive information are either quickly edited or shut down entirely. If you are online in China and want to access a site like Wikipedia that might have content offensive to the government, you will find your access blocked.

Repeated attempts to access the site, even if it's nothing more than the assumption on your part that the connection has a glitch or there's a temporary outage, may come to the attention of the authorities that will question your activities.

Some businessmen report instances of having left their hotel rooms only to come back to find their laptops and tablets in different places with evidence that attempts had been made to open programs and files.

While this sort of thing sounds like the plot of a cheap spy novel, it can and does happen in China. For this reason, be aware of what files you're bringing into the country and how any of the information might be misconstrued or seen as threatening in some way.

Physical Monitoring

In almost all large companies there will be at least one person at the senior executive level who is an appointee of the Communist Party. This individual's duty is to report on the activities of visitors and to keep the Party informed on their business dealings and strategies.

The government will want to know why you are in China and will expect to be told the purpose and content of your meetings. If you are provided with a driver, that person will likely be required to report on your round of activities.

If you meet with government officials, the interpreter will be a government employee. It may actually be a good precaution to take your own interpreter to ensure that nothing is lost in the translation and that you are provided with the complete content of all exchanges.

In some instances, you will be assigned an outright "handler" whose job it is to learn as much as possible about your business. It's even possible that the maids in your hotel are being paid to provide information based on what they see in your room!

There are many goals wrapped up in this kind of constant surveillance that create perceived benefit to the Chinese authorities:

- It allows the government to maintain its rigid control on the flow of information.

- The government's desire to learn all aspects of a foreigner's business goals and strategies are met.

- Industrial information is acquired that can be used for competitive purposes and to gain an advantage in any negotiations.

Surveillance is particularly overt for educators and researchers traveling to China. Young people of college age are traditionally the class most prone to developing dissident ideas, a potential the Chinese government will not allow to develop under any circumstance.

The Issue of Language

Since there are more English speakers in China than anywhere else in the world, many new importers cannot imagine that the "language barrier" is actually a problem. First, you must understand that there is not just one Chinese language.

In areas of southern China including Hong Kong, Cantonese is spoken, whereas Mandarin is the language of Northern China and Beijing. From region to region, however, the difference in how the language is spoken may be considerable.

There are two written forms of the language, traditional and simplified. The latter is used in mainland China, Singapore, and Malaysia. People who can read traditional Chinese can understand simplified, but the same is not true in reverse.

So, within the nation itself, you are not always dealing with people who completely understand one another, much less understand English at a vernacular level. Being fluent in a language is more than acquiring a working vocabulary.

You must understand the perceptions that form the culture's concept of communication to actually convey your ideas in a socially acceptable fashion.

English is a second language for the Chinese. They are speaking "our" language, but they are doing so from their own cultural mindset.

Learning English does not instantly alter their understandings of what constitutes either proper communication or good manners. To the Western ear, one can actually hinder the progress of the other!

Deductive vs. Inductive Communication

In the West, a topic is introduced and then discussed in a deductive manner. In the East, the process is more inductive. In order to be appropriately polite, reasons and explanations must be offered that preface any actual statement or request that is germane to the main topic.

This way of speaking can seem incredibly circuitous to the Western ear, which is not nearly so tuned to the context in which the communication is occurring.

I'll discuss more about the differences in American and Chinese culture shortly, but first let me suggest some basic principles of communication.

- Posing more questions to seek additional information is a standard approach in the West, and can work well in China, but only if it is done in the spirit of earnestly trying to understand and fix "the problem."

- Don't ask the same question over and over again seeking confirmation or you will convey the message that you do not believe what is being said to you.

- The frank expression of opinions, including making outright demands, is considered both insulting and uncomfortable in Chinese culture.

You cannot deal with a Chinese person without first establishing a relationship of trust. This means understanding levels of communication well beyond the spoken word.

The Importance of Context

Westerners use a minimal degree of context in our exchanges, taking words at their face value and not paying attention to factors like perceived status or body language. These things are, however, extremely important to the Chinese.

Our understanding of context is usually limited to any microcosm we inhabit, and might best be described as verbal shorthand.

Families, for instance, have their own language that is built on private and cultural allusions. An exchange that is based on contextual references can convey rich meaning, but only if you are privy to the context.

We can easily use a descriptive like "frustrated" or "lonely" to describe two young people who are forbidden to marry because their families dislike one another.

But, in a contextually based communication style, to refer to "Romeo and Juliet on the balcony," brings all the star-crossed love and longing of the situation to the description — *if you've seen or read Shakespeare's play.*

The Chinese do this kind of thing constantly in conversation, using proverbs and famous quotations to convey nuances of meanings.

There is also a tremendous amount of cultural obfuscation in an effort to be polite. Rather than say no, for instance, they will demur ambiguously, saying more study or research is needed to arrive at a decision.

Humor Gone Wrong

Humor in particular is highly contextual, and can be an absolute minefield in a cross-cultural setting. Jokes rely on idioms and popular vernacular that can rarely be rendered successfully in translation.

My best suggestion is to avoid trying to be funny. Your joke will fall flat and you'll be left with a horridly uncomfortable atmosphere that may not be salvageable. Try instead to just be courteous and pleasant.

Hire Translators and Interpreters

Since English is a second and maybe even a third language for Chinese businessmen (many are also fluent in Japanese and Russian), get all manufacturing instructions and specifications in Chinese.

Hire a technical translator to explain the information you have received and to help you craft appropriate replies. Make certain that you get a written report on these translated communications for your files. Some companies insist that contracts be delivered in both languages to ensure there are no misunderstandings.

The Concept of Guanxi

When business is conducted in Western countries, the order of the meeting is fairly standard. You make an appointment, show up on time, exchange a few pleasantries, hand out business cards, maybe drink a cup of coffee or tea, and then the deal is on the table.

Within a few minutes, a couple of hours on the outside, everyone knows if there's a chance to do business. You generally walk out with the sense that you've "closed" some aspect of the arrangement, or at least have a clear vision of what will happen next.

If you handle business in China in that fashion, you'll be referred to as a "seagull" and you won't get much — if anything — accomplished. Swooping in and ignoring all the social conventions of the Chinese business culture is the worst mistake you can make as an importer.

"Network of Relations"

Business dealings in China are built around the concept of "guanxi," (gwon-chee) which translates roughly as "network of relations," but again, this is not networking in the sense of how we network in the Western World. Guanxi is not an issue of just getting on Facebook or asking someone to accept your LinkedIn invitation.

The Chinese work in a world of carefully crafted trust relationships that rely on the right connections and the ability to ask for favors. Such relationships take time to build and the cultivation requires a great deal more than just formal business meetings.

When you are conducting business in China, you'll be socializing with the people with whom you *hope* to close a deal. If you're lucky and things go fairly "quickly," you'll have enough guanxi within a year to be regarded as a person worthy of trust.

Refining and Maintaining Guanxi

Once you've acquired your guanxi, you're faced with refining and maintaining it. There's no resting on your laurels. It's much easier to lose trust in the Chinese business culture than it is to gain it in the first place.

It's difficult for us in the West to understand that guanxi carries with it a social commitment that conveys the right to seek favors, for instance a key introduction to a valuable source.

When an introduction is made by a person who knows both of the parties, that, too, carries with it a level of commitment. The person making the introduction becomes part of the supporting network of the ongoing business relationship.

This is so outside our Western understanding of the way business is done, you will likely be better off hiring a sourcing broker or even an international procurement office to give you the guanxi you need to successfully enter the China marketplace in person.

If you don't go this route, you could be faced with traveling to China regularly in order to not only cultivate, but also maintain and grow your guanxi. And even if you do not go over often, you'll be expected to stay connected and to send business mementos that are thoughtfully selected.

If one of your China contacts calls you and asks that you help a relative of theirs who is coming to the states to study, you should never ignore the request.

You should send greetings on major Chinese holidays and answer all emails personally, and not in a perfunctory manner.

When these kinds of interactions don't come naturally or instinctively to you, hiring a consultant to prompt you to take the right actions is money well spent.

Never underestimate the vital role of cultivating and maintaining these crucial business relationships. If you want to successfully conduct business in China, nothing is more important than guanxi.

Ceremonial Etiquette

Interactions in China are based on ceremonial observances that must not be ignored. I've already touched briefly on the matter of business cards, which the Chinese see not as a piece of paper, but an extension of your person.

When you receive a business card, you should study it respectfully and put it away properly, not in your back pocket or casually tossed in your briefcase!

Always take small gifts for the individuals with whom you will be meeting. Make sure the item is thoughtful, but neutral in meaning.

Do not hug. Shake hands or bow. Wear a suit and tie to business meetings and business casual for dinners.

Dinner and drinks are a mandatory part of the process. If you do not drink, explain this in simple terms and ask for tea or a soda. Use the same approach for any dietary choices, like vegetarianism.

Almost everyone smokes, which may require patience on your part. Breathing in second-hand smoke is unpleasant, but essentially inevitable in your desire not to give offense.

Important Points to Remember

- Don't assume or convey the assumption that you're smarter than the person with whom you're negotiating or dealing.

- Remember that the art of listening and an air of courteous humility are valued in Chinese culture.

- Do not lose sight of the fact that you are a guest in another country. Neither criticism nor judgment is appropriate. This extends to the food, politics, and certainly to religion!

- Arguing is the height of bad manners. Debate will not be welcome in China. If you have a different opinion, then explain the situation from a new angle. This will convey to your host that you are not in agreement. Never create a situation where your host loses face. They must always have the option of stepping back with dignity. Learn to bargain instead of arguing.

- Do not make the mistake of thinking you're "in." You may have friends in China. You may conduct successful business deals there. You may put in supreme effort to learn the culture and even the language, but you will always be seen as what you are, a foreigner.

- Use your status as a foreigner to your advantage by being humble and openly acknowledging your ignorance of Chinese culture. This will not only smooth over the inevitable mistakes you will make, but your manners will be perceived as good for an outsider.

Chinese Culture and Women

In China, women are treated as equals, and face little to no discrimination. There is, however, an unusual shortage of women due to the "one-child policy" implemented in 1979.

This is not, however, the results of infanticide and abandonment as once was the case. Traditionally, sons were charged with the care and support of elderly parents, but couples desperate to have a boy are growing increasingly rare in Chinese culture.

Women who routinely do business in China report that their gender is a secondary perception to their role as "outsiders." In this context, they garner respect for their background, experience, authority, and business position and do not lose status because they are female.

As recently as the 1990s, both age and gender bias could hamper a person's ability to cultivate guanxi or "networking," but China has now become accustomed to seeing women in positions of authority. The natural tendency in all transactions is to concentrate on the person of authority, male or female, to the exclusion of gender.

Touring Factories

When you travel to China, it's extremely important to tour your supplier's manufacturing plant, and those of any other entity, like a contract manufacturer, with whom you're doing business.

This is not just a matter of jumping in the car with your driver and running out to the plant, however. You must prepare for your tour in advance. Think about what you want to see, what questions you want to ask, and how those questions should be framed.

Typically it's best to ask for an overview of the operation followed by a closer look at each individual step of the production process. Make sure you are there when the plant is actually in operation and people are working!

As you work on your questions and observations break them down into the component parts of the manufacturing process itself and take a written outline with you to the plant. At minimum spend 15-20 minutes in each major area of the facility. Make sure that you are accompanied by a translator who speaks the correct dialect.

You also need to verify in advance that the plant's management will be in attendance at the tour. The factory representative should be someone with adequate knowledge to answer your questions in detail.

In advance of the meeting, find out with whom you will be speaking. Get their title, role, and responsibilities. There is a tendency for people in China to assure you that they are "in charge," when in actuality, they are not. It's important that you are in fact dealing with a person of authority.

Find out the ownership and export focus of the factory. Facilities that produce for both the domestic and export marketplaces have a lower cost structure than exclusive export facilities and they have greater experience with quality standards on an international level.

On the other hand, while state-owned export factories are more expensive, they are more reliable and need less supervision from you.

At the plant on the day of your tour be sure to meet the entire management team and to exchange business cards with each member. Take the time to engage in small talk.

While the Chinese are getting to know you, you can observe how the management interacts with one another and with the workers. What is the level of interaction with "the boss?" Is the dynamic with the workers friendly and interactive?

Some of the things you will want to find out during your tour, either by observation or direct questioning:

- Are the facilities clean and up to date?
- Does the machinery seem to be well maintained?
- How is quality tracked and recorded?
- What software is used for process control?
- Are statistics gathered to drive planned improvements?
- How are waste products captured?
- What is the waste disposal process?
- What local and national reporting does the government require?

- Is material quality verifiable?
- What guarantees against toxic content, for instance lead in paint, can be provided?

You'll also need details on packaging, warehousing, and shipping. You want neat, tight packaging, and clean, dry warehousing and shipping. Ask for references, preferably from other Western companies doing business with the manufacturer(s).

Monitoring Factory Performance

As part of your working relationship with a China supplier, you will need ongoing methods of monitoring factory performance, not just in terms of output, but also in the ethical treatment of the workers.

The Chinese are incredibly industrious. Many factory laborers are determined to work their way up from generations of rural poverty. Although laws exist for the protection of the workers, this desire for advancement often outweighs potential legal ramifications.

Pair this with the constant pressure to drive prices down, and you have a climate ripe for factories to engage in deceptive and illegal practices.

Once you have established a relationship with a supplier, there should be additional tours in the future that may include the services of an auditor on site to avoid the common practice in China of keeping two sets of books.

The second set exists to hide the amount of overtime workers are actually putting in.

Chinese law allows 44-48 hours weekly with 12 hours of overtime. In reality, most workers put in 80 hours and take only Sunday afternoon off.

In order to verify good working conditions you can:

- Ask to audit payroll records.
- Speak to older workers who will tend to be more truthful.
- Give workers your business card and make it clear you are available.
- Verify the presence of safety features including unlocked windows and exits.

As part of your tour of the factory, you may also want to ask to see the dormitories where workers are housed to assess the living conditions. They will not be like those you would be used to seeing in the West, but you will still be able to get a good sense of worker treatment in this way.

Factory Audits

Auditing factory operations in China to ensure that international standards for human rights are honored is not as easy or straightforward as it might appear on the surface of things. Both the factory owners and the factory workers are in a position that is difficult for Westerners to completely understand.

If factory management engages in a policy of full disclosure, they run the risk of losing orders and having to lay off workers. The workers themselves actually do not want to be protected in the way workers in the West envision protection.

Chinese workers are driven to work as much as possible to escape the crushing burden of rural poverty for themselves and their families.

Your dilemma, however, is that of major brands like Target and Wal-Mart. Your business reputation can be irreparably harmed if you ignore all aspect of human rights and deal with products made in shadow factories whose operations are decried globally.

Issues of oversight are made somewhat easier in larger import operations. If you are a newcomer to importing, however, and are operating on a very small scale, you will have next to no control over the conditions at the factories where your products are made.

Chapter 7 – Let's Get Started

Everyone who buys a book of this nature wants to skip immediately to the chapter that says, "Let's Get Started." This is that chapter, but if you've opened the book and skipped to this point, I encourage you go back and read the preceding material.

"Importing from China" sounds so easy thanks to sites like Alibaba, that the phrase has almost become a buzzword in its own right.

If you have read the first six chapters of this book, you know there are many different shades of importing, and a great deal to understand about the Chinese themselves in order to be successful.

Yes, importing from China can be done exclusively online and your business can be run via email with sales taking place in venues like eBay and Amazon.

That does not, however, make importing a get rich quick scheme. Any business, to be truly viable and sustainable, requires work on your part, and a clear understanding of the business fundamentals.

What You Should Have Done Already

By this stage of the game, you should have conducted your niche and market research and selected a product that you can acquire from China at a greatly reduced cost and for which there is a solid market demand.

You should also have drafted a business plan that includes consideration of the following:

- An analysis of your proposed business venture in terms of strengths, weaknesses, opportunities, and threats.

- An analysis of your target market including age, gender, occupation, interest, and similar relevant factors.

- A consideration of your competitors and an idea of how you can gain the edge in the marketplace (i.e. price, availability, design, features).

- A projection of planned promotion, marketing, and advertising strategies.

- An outline of your business structure including where and how you will sell your items, and how they will be handled and shipped (include the supply chain and associated costs.)

- A complete financial projection including income and expense statements and cash flow projections.

Be sure that appropriate experts have critiqued your plan including non-competitors experienced in matters of international business as well as someone in finance like your banker or accountant.

Depending on how your business will be structured, you may need to do some or all of the following:

- Pick a business name and decide the form the business will take (for instance, sole proprietorship, corporation, or DBA.)

- Register your business for tax and licensing purposes and pay any applicable fees. This may or may not require the services of a CPA or attorney.

- Obtain any necessary permits or certificates for selling or reselling items.

- Apply for a Federal Tax ID number as applicable to the structure of your business.

Keep good records from the start, filing all paper work and electronic copies for ease of access. Find out what kinds of expenses are tax deductible and file those receipts in a separate location.

Consider an Import Consultant

Depending on the projected scope and long-term goals of your business, you may want to investigate working with an international trade consultant for the first few months.

Import-export consultants are quite easy to locate online, although if you can get a first-person referral to find someone reliable, that is ideal.

You can either search directly for import-export consulting companies, or use a site like Elance.com to find freelancers working in this area.

Should you go this route, be sure to look at the individual's performance rating on the site. Read reviews left for them by former clients. Ask for references and follow through on checking them out.

There is nothing to stop you from building your import business without the services of a consultant. If yours is a small start-up, you likely will not have the financial wherewithal to hire a consultant.

It is worth mentioning, however, that such an arrangement can be worth the investment to more quickly gain a working understanding of the business.

It is also possible that after experiencing initial success on your own, you may want to engage a consultant to help you take your business to the next level.

(Most consulting firms offer a free consultation to discuss the nature and scope of your business after which they will give you a custom quote for their fees.)

The Consultant's Role

The consultant's job is to work for you, but also with you. The best arrangement isn't a company that will do everything to the exclusion of helping you learn the ropes.

Make it clear when you are discussing hiring the company or the individual that you want to learn the importing business and gain the necessary experience to run your own venture.

This does not preclude continuing to work with the consultant in the future. It's common in larger importing businesses to hire trade consultants to serve in a managerial capacity.

Ownership of the Work Product

When you read the consulting contract, but sure that you are comfortable with the language in regard to work product.

All work completed and all information gained by the consultant belongs to you at the termination of the contract. It should be clear that both the work and the connections it entails are assets of your company.

Scope of the Consulting Activities

Be sure to find out the exact scope of the consulting services for which you are contracting. Professionals in this genre can be useful in day-to-day operations, but they are also helpful in identifying and choosing suppliers and even in securing international trade financing.

Although it may be hard for newcomers to know, try to hire a consultant that best matches your existing skill set. You only want to pay for help in areas where you are truly deficient or in need of expert instruction.

Pros and Cons of Consultants

There are both pros and cons to working with consultants. The firm or individual will (or certainly should) have existing contacts, know the culture, and be able to efficiently negotiate the language barrier.

The biggest con is, of course, the consulting fee, but you also have to be sure that the firm does not have a bias toward a particular manufacturer. Your goal is to have a consultant that will secure the optimum deal and best rates.

If the consultant will be representing you in person in China, it's preferable to have someone age 40 or older since the Chinese regard age as a mark of acquired wisdom.

Matters of Compliance

I do not pretend to be an expert in matters of import law, especially as they vary by country. Both laws and regulations are subject to change and can be affected by the current climate of international relations.

Research each product on a case-by-case basis. Never assume that only one law or one set of regulations applies to an individual product or that the item may not be subject to multiple enforcement codes.

There are no major restrictions placed on importing more consumable goods into the United States, but there may be other conditions that must be satisfied.

For instance, electronic devices in the U.S. must be compliant with FCC standards, but their power sources must meet Underwriters Laboratories (UL) standards.

Good sources to research specific items are the U.S. Customs site at www.cbp.gov and the HM Revenue and Customs site for the UK at www.hmrc.gov.uk.

You must also pay attention to the chain of regulations if you are going to re-export items. A device that meets the FCC standard in the United States will not be eligible for sale in Western Europe where the standards set by the CE marking will be necessary.

By the same token a power supply that carries the U.S. "UL" label will need a "C-UL" label to be sold in Canada.

Creating Your Brand

What many beginning importers don't realize is that you are creating a *brand* with the products you buy and sell. There has to be a way for the market to find you and to know who you are. You must create an identity that you can market along with your products.

Product Identity

It difficult to over-emphasize the importance of branding, but the power of this essential business strategy is easy to explain. Go into any grocery store and ask a shopper why he or she is buying one type of product over another. You will likely be met with a blank stare and a reply along the lines of, "Because this is the one my Mom bought."
From childhood we are conditioned to think that all facial tissues are Kleenex®, or that all soda is Coca-Cola®. Truly powerful brands become the definition of what it means to *be* a particular product in the minds of consumers.

Some new importers scoff and say, "I'm too small to be worried about creating a brand." Nothing could be farther from the truth. Businesses of all sizes and types acquire their products from third parties and brand them. This isn't an optional strategy; it's a critical one.

Don't make the mistake of thinking of yourself as just a middleman. Anyone can acquire and resell products "as is." There are lots of people doing it on sites like eBay and Amazon, but the ones that stand out have an identity that makes them noticeable to potential customers.

Logos and Packaging

Hire a graphic designer to create a logo for your products and invest in packaging that showcases both the item and its identity.

The best practice is to have your products arrive to you from the manufacturer in your branded packaging with your company name and logo in place.

As part of the agreement you make with the supplier, you should provide them with packaging specifications and the correct graphic files to accurately reproduce your company name and logo. You will want to both approve the product and the packaging before ordering in large quantities. Make certain that the manufacturer does not put its company name anywhere on either the product or the packaging.

While it is certainly possible to acquire your products from one company and to have them packaged at another, in my opinion that creates nothing but a headache for you in terms of your supply chain and shipping.

You certainly don't want to be in a position where you're sitting in your basement packing your own products! For the sake of consistency and price control, try to get everything done in one smooth assembly process.

Selling Your Products Online

Many beginning importers acquire their products through online sources and also place the items on selling sites like eBay, Rakuten, and Amazon among others. It is also common for importers to have their own websites.

With well-researched niches and good products with a strong identity, selling online can be a highly successful business either as extra money on the side or as a full-time endeavor.

The key to selling in this way is to diversify, placing your products on as many sites as possible. Never base your business on the continued presence of a single selling platform. If the platform goes away, your business goes with it!

The factors to consider in listing with any site include:

- registration fees
- listing fees
- commissions charged
- shipping

Each of these elements affects both the price for which you must list your item, and the amount of profit you can earn from each sale. These margins will vary by selling site.

You should track your sales and margins for each site, preferably in a spreadsheet. Remember that rarely are any two sales equal when you work across multiple selling platforms.

Put your time and energy into the ones where your products are getting maximum exposure and customer interest while generating the highest profits.

(Please note that the following information in regard to fees and percentages was accurate at the time of this writing, but all such policies are subject to change.)

Your Own Site

Without question, listing your products on your own site gives you the maximum amount of control and negates the need to pay listing fees or seller commissions.

The challenges in achieving visibility in Google rankings are fairly large, however, unless you have a marketing budget that will allow you to drive traffic via ads and other linking strategies.

Frankly, Google does not make it easy for small business owners to drive traffic, and you will have to have some type of shopping cart and a merchant account to take credit card orders.

There are, of course, lower cost options for taking payments, like PayPal, but you will be in charge of handling all shipping and returns on your own. Fees can rapidly eat into your profits, and there's a lot of headache in administering and updating your website.

It is for this reason that more "turnkey" solutions like the following sites are so popular with online sellers. They do all involve fees, but those can be factored into your business plan. The predictability of such fee structures is also useful in scaling your operations and setting sales goals.

eBay

When you are selling products you have imported on eBay, your best option is not to auction them, but rather to list the items for a fixed price. Your listing will still appear in searches performed by buyers, but there is no chance for your product to undersell for pennies on the dollar.

You do not have to have a specific "feedback" score to list items at a fixed price, and the minimum price allowed is $.99. Ebay offers a fee calculator at:

www.fees.ebay.com/feeweb/feecalculator

This will allow you to calculate both listing and shipping fees, which you can then standardize. You can set your listing up to indicate how many of the items you have in stock and then re-supply it after X number of sales.

Although a monthly cost is involved, you will likely want to open an eBay "store" where you can maintain constant listings of all the products in your inventory. You can learn more about eBay stores at:

pages.ebay.com/help/sell/storefees.html

There are many nuances to maintaining fixed priced listings. Do not, for instance, "over supply" the listing. If you say you have 100 items, the buyer will not sense any urgency to get the product before it's gone.

If you say you have only 5, they will be more likely to buy immediately because they believe the supply is limited.

Never underestimate the power of psychology in making a sale. Buyer desire and perception of scarcity or uniqueness are powerful motivators.

Do not make the mistake of letting your listed supply of an item fall to zero or you'll have to re-enter the entire listing. This is not only an administrative inconvenience, but also a poor management strategy in terms of visibility within the eBay search engine.

EBay gives higher search engine placement to items that have sold. If you've sold 30 units of any one item in a single listing, you'll appear higher up in search results for that item.

It's also likely that some users who are dithering about their purchase have decided to "watch" your listing. If you let the inventory fall to zero and the listing is deleted, you will lose those potential customers.

Chapter 7 – Let's Get Started

Learning to sell effectively on eBay is something of an art form in and of itself. If you are planning to do a lot of business there, I recommend that you study the ecosphere and really learn how to maximize the potential of the marketplace.

EBay used to be a place where people got rid of their old junk and traded in "collectibles." The site has evolved into the Internet's premier marketplace after Amazon with as many or more listings of new items at fixed prices.

It's worth your time and energy to educate yourself about the fine points of selling on eBay in order to leverage your share of those potential buyers.

Rakuten

Rakuten was founded in 1997 and is the largest e-commerce site in Japan. It is also one of the biggest Internet companies in the world with annual sales of more than $4 billion. In 2013, Rakuten bought Buy.com for $250 million and renamed it "Rakuten.com Shopping."

The site is often waggishly referred to as the "biggest e-commerce site you haven't heard of." It is definitely a place you want to list your products and is equally as important as eBay and Amazon.

Registration is free, and there are no fees for listing items, but you must have a tax identification number and valid credit card and checking account information to complete the process of signing up. Commissions range from 5% to 15% and are charged at the time a sale is completed.

The company provides a comprehensive seller's guide at:

www.rakuten.com/loc/Marketplace-Sellers-Guide/65546.html

Amazon

You can sell on Amazon as either a company with a "store" or an individual. If you plan to sell as a "professional," you will be charged $39.99 per month.

Listings include pictures and descriptions of the items, with the ability to tag each product for better placement in internal searches by users. Commissions range from 8% to 15%, varying by product.

Some types of products require sellers to apply for approval, including, but not limited to clothing, luggage, and major appliances. In early 2014, Amazon was not reviewing any further applications for jewelry sellers.

Typically when Amazon restricts applications for sales in a given area the products in questions have received high levels of customer complaints, been the subject of fraud, or exhibit an unusually high level of returns.

Amazon is interested in working with legitimate sellers, so all applications are an effort to verify these facts and maintain high levels of quality for the given items.

As a potential seller, go to the "General Help" section at Amazon.com and look under the sub-section for "Policies and Agreements."

The topic for "Category, Product, and Listing Restrictions" will help you to determine which of your products you can sell with Amazon.

(Building a positive selling history with non-restricted items will improve your reputation with Amazon and increase the likelihood that you can successfully enter the restricted categories in the future.)

Chapter 7 – Let's Get Started

If you work through "Fulfillment by Amazon" (FBA), you will ship your product to an Amazon warehouse where it will then be offered to the buyer at discounted UPS rates.

This is an attractive option since Amazon handles all aspects of cataloging, storing, shipping, and tracking your items once they are received at the warehouse. They also take care of managing any returns.

There are no upfront charges to have your products handled via FBA, but the commissions charged are close to 20%, which is much higher than other platforms. The actual rate of commission is factored according to:

- product weight and dimensions
- quantity ordered
- presence of other items in the order

Most items purchased through FBA are eligible for free shipping if they are part of orders that total $35 or above.

Obviously FBA is a huge advantage in scaling your business, but never have your products shipped directly from your supplier to Amazon. Receive the products yourself for inspection and then send them to the Amazon warehouse.

Not only is this a matter of quality control, but there have also been instances of Amazon locating manufacturers on high sale items and purchasing the items directly. High search rankings capture the company's attention, and they will go after a larger share of your business than what they can receive on commissions.

Amazon maintains a complete seller's resource center at services.amazon.com/content/seller-resources-how-to-guides.htm

iOffer

Based out of San Francisco, California, iOffer.com was founded in 2002. It works somewhat like eBay, but the listed prices are fixed, with no auctions in the mix.

Sellers list products free of charge, with fees calculated at variable rates according to sales price. In almost all instances, the fees are lower than those you would pay for an eBay fixed price listing.

The site integrates listings from your eBay account and shows your feedback there, which increases your exposure without the need to create additional listings.

For more information on iOffer, see the company's Frequently Asked Questions for sellers at:

www.ioffer.com/help/selling_faq

Again, while this is one of the lesser known of the online selling sites, iOffer still lists millions of products and is a good marketplace for niche products.

Managing Barcodes

If you work through some retail sites, including Amazon, your products must have a barcode or UPC, a fact that draws many new importers up short. This is not so major a hurdle as you might think.

You can easily purchase your barcodes at sites like www.nationwidebarcode.com.

The codes you purchase are yours to use as long as you like, and can be printed on label sheets and affixed to your items or emailed to your supplier for direct integration in your packaging.

You will need one unique barcode per product.

Advantages of Sales Portals

There are numerous advantages to be gained from working with any of the large online sales portals like eBay and Amazon.

Price Control

Even with the required fees and commissions, you still control prices within your brand. This is far preferable to working through resellers who purchase your products and set their own prices. I am an advocate of retaining control at as many levels in the process as possible.

Working with resellers can easily create a situation where you are in competition with your own products, which devalues what you are selling in the eyes of your customers.

Cost Control

In a situation where you know what fees are associated with the listing, selling, and shipping of your products, you have a better set of guidelines to curb prices in other areas.

You can judge when to spend money on your business, and make changes and additions only when profits warrant the upgrade. In the beginning, for instance, you can store your products in your spare bedroom or garage rather than pay for space in a warehouse or other facility.

By controlling fixed costs, you can judge discretionary expenses like hiring employees, or opting to automate certain parts of your operation.

Targeted Product Expansion

Working across multiple sales portals, you will have good benchmarks to judge how and when to expand your product line.

It's a mistake to sell a wide variety of products in the beginning. If you misjudge the market, you'll get stuck with excess inventory. Your first sales will give you much greater insight into the niche you're attempting to work.

Sales portals will also help you to refine your product branding and marketing, and give you accurate metrics to compare year to year or in high sales seasons. They are also excellent venues for testing new products so you can keep your catalog of items robust and profitable.

Monitor Changing Margins

With the ability to track your numbers accurately, you can set sales goals and also watch your margins. If your product costs go up, you can adjust your selling price or decide to phase out the product or model in favor of another, more profitable item.

Margins are always the bottom line in importing. If you're not tripling your investment on imported items going to retailers, or doubling them on "flips" destined for liquidators, you need to rethink all your numbers.

Anticipate Holiday Spikes

Working with sales portals also lets you anticipate holiday spikes more accurately, and take advantage of heavy sales days that are not available in the "real" retail world.

It's a given that sales in physical retail venues increase from the middle of November to Christmas Eve, and that Black Friday, the day after Thanksgiving, is a huge sales day. So huge, in fact, you couldn't drag me to a mall on that day. But when you are selling online, you will also benefit from Cyber Monday, which is the Monday after Thanksgiving.

Sales on that day average $1.5 billion, and are especially strong for items that make good gifts.

Many online sellers see double and triple sales for the month based on that one day alone. Knowing this, you can anticipate your inventory needs based on year-over-year sales and be prepared to meet demand.

Customer Service

Strive to provide your buyers the best customer service experience possible. Too many companies neglect customer service and it shows.

Include a card or sheet of paper in every order that has an email address and/or phone number where your customers can reach you if they have any questions or problems.

Respond to customer emails as soon as possible—within an hour is best. This lends confidence to potential customers and shows existing customers that you stand behind your product. Offer 100% money back guarantees.

By giving your customers a sense that they can trust you, you give them peace of mind and make them more willing to come back to you for repeat orders.

Selling items of excellent quality and standing by your products is the best way to keep returns at a bare minimum. Also, never forget that customers love fast shipping and will often be willing to pay a little more for something they know they can get quickly.

If at all possible – and it should be completely possible – get orders out within 24 hours of the time they are placed. Actually, same day shipping is even better, especially when you are working via eBay and Amazon where building a reputation via customer feedback is crucial.

Chapter 8 – Shipping Options from China

Shipping may be the most challenging and potentially stressful aspect of importing. In basic terms, your choices boil down to airfreight and sea freight, but the specifics of those choices as they relate to customs and duties are much, much more complicated.

In general, however, you should only use airfreight to get your samples faster for evaluation purposes. Sea freight is the cheaper option for actual shipment of products, but it is much slower and requires more planning on your part.

Also understand that with sea freight you don't pay for door-to-door delivery. Your goods are not going to just leave the factory in China and arrive on your doorstep.

The shipment will be delivered to a warehouse in your vicinity and you must arrange pick up within 5 days. After that time, daily storage fees apply. Importers who don't understand these fine details lose a lot of money well before their products ever reach them.

Once you have your shipping routine in place and have successfully completed a couple of shipments, everything becomes easier and more comprehensible, but I'll be honest, those first couple of shipments can be agonizing and completely overwhelming.

Because I've been through the ordeal myself, I would not recommend attempting your initial shipments on your own. If I were starting out again, I would absolutely work with a freight forwarder and a customs broker.

Freight forwarding companies handle the required documents for clearing customs and they understand the confusing language of international trade referred to as Incoterms.

When I negotiated my first shipment, the alphabet soup of Incoterms alone had me reaching for my bottle of antacids.

What are Incoterms?

Incoterms are three letter codes that define who is burdened with specific transportation costs and other risks involved in the international movement of goods. Some of the most common are EXW, FOB, CFR, and CIF.

EXW (Ex Works)

In this scenario, the importer is responsible for arranging to have the goods picked up from the factory in China and delivered to their destination, covering all costs in between. Important factors to consider are the distance from the factory to the port, and the size of the shipment.

FOB (Free on Board)

With this shipping arrangement, the supplier pays to have the goods loaded on a ship in China and covers the local transportation costs and the costs to clear the items for export. The importer pays for the sea freight and the applicable customs, taxes, and domestic import on his end.

CFR / CIF

Cost and Freight (CFR) and Cost Insurance and Freight (CIF) are essentially the same thing except for the obvious fact that one includes the cost of insurance and one does not. In both cases, the supplier pays the cost of getting the shipment from their location to the port of your choice.

Understanding Duties

The amount of duty charged depends on the type of goods and their country of origin. All products are classified under the Harmonized System of tariff codes, which are used in determining duty rates.

Chapter 8 – Shipping Options from China

This is a huge database that includes a code for just about every item you can possibly imagine, but harmonized codes are not as cut and dry as you might think.

It's often possible to get customs to agree to classify your product in a different way for the express purpose of achieving a lower duty. This is called getting a letter of ruling, a scenario I described in the Foreword of this book.

If you haven't read that section, you may want to flip back and do so now. In brief, however, this is the story I shared. By getting a letter of ruling defining a shipment of candles without wicks as "wax" rather than as "candles," a very smart importer was able to save $14,000 in duties per container!

Not only are your duty rates affected by how your products are classified, they are also set according to the country of origin for the shipment. Governments classify other nations as enemies, friends, or best friends, which affects how trade relationships are handled.

Goods from an enemy nation like North Korea will be charged duty percentages in the high double digits, whereas best friends like Canada and the U.S. maintain a free trade agreement.

Most countries are simply "friends," which is rather misleadingly referred to as "Most Favored Nations." For such countries, duty rates typically fall in the range of 10% or less.

Customs Brokers

The form importers must fill out to pay duties is, frankly, incredibly intimidating, requiring the correct tariff code, country of origin, and invoice value. Be honest about the invoice value! Shipments are audited randomly, and fines are steep.

Like many aspects of importing, you can do these things yourself, and you certainly should understand the process, however, it's really best to work with a customs broker, especially for your first shipment.

Brokers charge $100 to $300 plus applicable taxes and duties, but they are experts at filling out customs declarations forms and resolving any issues that arise.

These professionals will literally save your sanity and keep you from getting so discouraged you run screaming from the idea of ever importing another shipment of goods.

Summary Thoughts on Shipping

In determining how you will handle shipping your products, you must be guided by the size and scope of your business. Shipping considerations can be scaled up and down, as you will see in the next chapter on Legal Considerations.

If you are an "arm chair" importer bringing in small lots of this or that widget for sale primarily on eBay, your shipping will likely still occur by airfreight and costs will be negligible due to the low volume with which you're dealing. Getting 500 computer styli that can be shipped in something smaller than a shoebox is very different than a shipping container of engine parts.

If you are a larger importer facing complex matters of freight movement, customs clearances, and duty calculation, work with professionals for your first few shipments until you have a replicable, streamlined shipment process in place.

Chapter 9 - Legal Considerations

This text does not purport to offer a comprehensive legal treatment of all the laws and regulations that apply to importing goods into the United States or the United Kingdom, but the following areas are things you need to consider.

In the end, you may opt to work with a customs agent or broker, or to seek legal advice in any of these areas. The following commentary is intended merely to introduce the topics and to offer fundamental explanations.

U.S. Customs: Informal vs. Formal Entry

Imported commercial items in the United States qualify for informal entry under customs law if they cost less than $2,500. There is no need to post a customs bond, file customs paperwork, or use a broker.

If the items cost $2,500 or more, the entry must be formal with upfront cash, a posted bond, and paperwork filed with the Customers and Border Protection. If these requirements are not met, you won't be able to pick up your imported merchandise.

Formal entry is tedious and really should involve the services of a customs broker. There are exceptions to the $2,500 threshold, notably textiles, which require brokers and bonding for amounts totaling $250 and more.

Informal Entry Preferred

If at all possible, go with informal entry even if it means smaller, multiple shipments. Avoiding the broker and bond charges and the procedural burden of formal entry is worth arranging three $2,000 shipments in a month as opposed to a single $6,000 shipment.

Don't try to cheat by getting your manufacturer to write a false, low dollar amount on the paperwork. If you get caught, the fine will be steep. The only cost added to informal entry shipments is the import tariff, which you will pay through your carrier or shipping company.

U.S. Tariffs and Ruling Letters

Tariffs or duties are taxes levied on imported goods. All products you import are subject to tariff payments, but the amount can be a gray area. For this reason, it's worth your time to have a free ruling letter on product classifications created by U.S. Customs and Border Protection for your imported items.

Take this step before you actually import the items. The letter is permanent and legally binding. In the event of a future dispute, the letter will be an authoritative tariff classification. To obtain a ruling letter, apply at:

http://www.cbp.gov/xp/cgov/trade/legal/rulings/eRulingRequirements.xml.

Give your manufacturer copies of the ruling letter for inclusion in every shipment to keep the importation process as smooth and seamless as possible.

Protecting Your Brand Online

It is not uncommon for established sellers with well-crafted brands on sites like eBay or Amazon to be forced to deal with unscrupulous competitors. In an effort to sell lesser quality copies of products at lower rates, these individuals steal your listing photos and copyrighted branding.

The first step to stop such infringement is a cease and desist email to the seller asking that the purloined material be removed within 48 hours. If the other seller does not comply, your next recourse is through the Amazon compliance department or the eBay Verified Rights Owner (VeRO) program.

For the process of reporting a listing on eBay see:

pages.ebay.com/help/tp/vero-rights-owner.html

On Amazon see:

www.amazon.com/gp/help/reports/infringement

There is no need to formally register either the Copyright Designation © or the trademark designation ™ to use these marks on your listings and photos. You cannot, however, apply the federal registration symbol ® without formal registration at www.uspto.gov.

U.S. State Sales Tax

If you maintain a physical presence in one of the states in the United States, you are required to collect and to pay sales tax. Visit your home state's department of revenue website to determine the exact procedures that apply.

As an example, however, if your business is based in New York, you are bound by law to collect sales tax on all shipments made to customers and locations in that state.

UK Importing Regulations

Importers in the UK must have an Economic Operator Registration and Identification (EORI) number. The necessary application form may be obtained at customs.hmrc.gov.uk/eorischeme and submitted via email to eori@hmrc.gsi.gov.uk.

For both imports and exports of goods a full declaration is required on the C88 Single Administration Document (SAD). Once the form is submitted and accepted, the required duties must be paid before the goods can be released.

Every entry of goods receives an individual "Entry Number" and importers are given the "Entry Acceptance Advice," which is a record of the submissions and acceptance of the declaration.

Chapter 9 - Legal Considerations

For complete information on the applicable tax obligations, see www.gov.uk/starting-to-import. The same page contains material on export controls and licenses.

The different charges that can be applied to imported goods depending on their type include, but are not limited to:

- customs duty
- import VAT
- excise duty
- anti-dumping duty
- Common Agricultural Policy (CAP) charges.

These amounts typically are considered due at the point at which Customs actually accepts the import and are paid via a "Deferment Account," check, bank draft, BACS or CHAPS. You can find more information on this topic at www.gov.uk/duty-relief-for-imports-and-exports.

Importers are required to keep accurate records of all international trading activity including accurate customs declarations that reflect the accurate value, origin, and classification of the goods in question.

The following supporting documents should also be maintained:

- original orders
- invoices
- delivery notes
- credit and debit notes
- any import and/or export documents

- payment records and receipts
- ledgers and journals
- bills of landing
- airway bills
- certificates of shipment

Keep these documents for four years and any records relative to VAT for six years. To find more extensive information on required business records see:
www.hmrc.gov.uk/factsheet/record-keeping.pdf

Afterword

Hopefully you can now see why I said in the beginning that the definitive book on importing from China is something of an impossibility. Any healthy business climate is dynamic in nature, implying change and evolution over time.

The China market is expanding in pace with the nation's growing role on the international stage. Both laws and attitudes will change in response, within China and outside her borders.

This fact alone means Western businessmen must approach their dealings in China with flexibility and a willingness to adapt. Failure to do so will, in my opinion, doom any importing endeavor over the long term.

Throughout this text, I have tried to deal with issues of scalability. I am well aware that there are many people who now make their living by working from home through various online channels for consulting and commerce.

One layer of importing from China fits this "stay at home" model. Sites like Alibaba make it possible for armchair entrepreneurs to research product niches, acquire reasonably small shipments from China, and sell the items via online sales portals like Amazon and eBay. This is essentially what I did when I imported earrings.

Afterword

I also had my own site at the time, and had more than my fair share of fighting Google for good search rankings. Every time the search engine changed its algorithms, I found myself in high adjustment mode. Still, I handled it all from the comfort of my home on my laptop. It was a good way to do business and I enjoyed sound profit margins.

When I switched to importing my own branded jigsaw puzzles, things got more complicated and I found myself negotiating the often-murky waters of shipping costs, customs clearance, and duty payments.

I assure you I made a lot of mistakes and endured many headaches, for the simple reason that I didn't take as much time as I should have to understand the basics of importing – including how to effectively negotiate with my Chinese counterparts.

My goal in this book is to give you a broad overview of the importing process with an eye toward refining your initial planning. By working through some fundamental steps, you should be able to save yourself from some of those same headaches.

Beginning with a complete, written business plan, a solid niche and product research are essential. If you don't do those things and just plunge blindly ahead, you're in for a rocky road.

While everyone wants to save money, there are steps along the way where spending a little on professional advice and guidance will make your long-term prospects more

Afterword

profitable. Again, this is a matter of scale, but if you cannot stay below the informal entry customs level, get help!

I would also counsel you to be a constant student of importing. In the Relevant Websites section that follows, I've given you a list of sites online where you can stay current with what is happening in the world of importing.

Read a lot of "expert" viewpoints and take away what seems most relevant to your personal experience. I'm not a big fan of gurus and I don't purport to be one, but I spend part of each morning catching up on the news in my various business "worlds."

I'm a firm believer that complacency is the enemy to forward thinking success. Remember the story I told about the guy who imported the plastic sleeves that he thought would be used by photographers for their proofs?

He had completely missed out on the digital photo revolution and narrowly missed getting stuck with thousands of clear plastic bags. Thankfully he was able to quickly do some market research and place his product with craft enthusiasts.

The point, however, is that he should have done his research first, not gone on his 20-year-old experience as a one-time wedding photographer.

You can't afford to miss out on trends that will affect the popularity and profitability of your products! Tracking popular culture and technological innovation are all part of being an importer. Those things are an aspect of market anticipation.

It's both a skill and a talent, but neither can come into play on your behalf if you don't keep your head up and your attention trained on the world around you.

Frankly, these are the things that I think make importing fun. I've been an entrepreneur since I was a kid selling magazine subscriptions and trading baseball cards for resale. I like to make money, but in the process, I like to feel that my intellect and native talents are being challenged.

Importing from China will certainly do that for you and more. If you approach the endeavor as a business, not as a get rich quick scheme, you can turn importing into a profitable sideline or a full-time business.

Regardless, I wish you the best of luck. Confucius said, "The will to win, the desire to succeed, the urge to reach your full potential . . . these are the keys that will unlock the door to personal excellence."

I wish you excellent success with importing and hope that you will succeed and reach your full potential in a business sector ripe with opportunities at virtually every level.

Relevant Websites

Importing From China – Blog
http://chineseimporting.com/

Duty Calculator
http://www.dutycalculator.com/country-guides/Import-duty-taxes-when-importing-into-China

China Source and Supply
http://www.chinasourceandsupply.com/

Alibaba
http://www.alibaba.com/

Global Sources
http://www.GlobalSources.com/

Hong Kong Suppliers and Manufactures
http://www.hkdc.com/

US Customs and Border Protection – Licenses / Permits
https://help.cbp.gov/app/answers/detail/a_id/197/~/importing---licenses%2Fpermits

UK Customs
http://www.hmrc.gov.uk/customs/

Business News Daily
http://www.businessnewsdaily.com/3297-importing-from-china.html

Alcohol and Tobacco Tax and Trade Bureau International Trade Division
http://www.ttb.gov/itd/china.shtml

Frequently Asked Questions

There are so many potential "frequently asked questions" in regard to importing, I almost hesitated to include this section. Here are a few things I am asked fairly often, but I assure you, for every one of these questions, there are 50 more.

As you're reading my book and then moving deeper into your study of importing, I recommend keeping a notebook of terms and questions. Ultimately you will become conversant in all these confusing concepts, but it can take time.

What are harmonized codes?

The Harmonized Commodity Coding System is a universally accepted tariff classification system. The codes are comprised of 6-10 digits and allow countries to identify goods for the administration of customs programs and the collection of trade data.

Harmonized or HS codes are used to set tariff and tax rates on imported goods. China uses a 10-digit system of codes for both imports and exports.

What is a tariff schedule?

Tariff schedules are regularly published by nations to make available their HS codes, rates for import tariffs, and additional information like regulatory measures and rates for such things as:

- value-added tax (VAT)
- import consumption tax
- export tariff
- and any other applicable charges

Tariff schedules are typically set in place for a year at a time. Up-to-date tariff schedules are available from governmental trade commissions.

This all sounds complicated. How can I understand tariffs and duties?

Obviously you can sit down and study tariff and import law, but that is incredibly time consuming and not your real focus for wanting to get into the import business.

I recommend that as part of your first major shipments from China you work with freight forwarders and import brokers.

These entities are professionals in moving goods internationally and negotiating complicated customs and tariff laws. You can learn a great deal from them, making their fees well worth it.

Small importers who can stay below the "formal" customs level (which is under $2500 in the United States) will likely not have to go this route, but mid-level to major importers should always hire consultants at least in the beginning.

Over time, you will get a set shipping chain in place and likely even have specific ruling letters for your products to avoid customs snarls, but as an importing "newbie" all of these things can seem like landmines waiting to go off in your face.

Can't I do all of my importing from my laptop at home?

On one level, yes, you can do everything necessary to import goods from China online. This very moment you can pop over to Alibaba.com, browse the marketplace, find a supplier, negotiate a deal, and in a few weeks be the proud owner of X number of widgets imported from China.

- But can you sell those widgets?
- Is there a demand for the widgets?
- Are the widgets well made?
- Were they manufactured according to specifications acceptable in a Western market?
- Did you get a competitive price?
- Did you work with a reputable seller?
- Can you acquire more of the same product?
- Have you considered where you will do your selling?
- Do you know what your profit margins will be?

And those are just a few of the questions you should be able to answer!

If you are going to be a successful importer, there's no getting around doing your market niche and product research. If you are going to use an online marketplace like Alibaba, you have to learn how to navigate in that environment and avoid being scammed. Signing up is easy; being smart in the market is complicated.

I'm not trying to discourage you from being a small importer, but don't think it's as simple as just ordering the products. You still need to learn the same fine points of importing and of Chinese business culture as the person who will be bringing in large containers of items for resale to major retailers.

Is Chinese business culture hard to understand?

Yes and no. Intellectually, most of us can understand Chinese business culture after reading some basic guidelines, but overcoming our instinctual cultural responses to basic matters of etiquette and communication are much harder.

To the Western mind it seems that Chinese business deals are overly formalized and proceed at a glacial pace. It's difficult to understand the cultural and historical underpinnings of such dealings or the extent to which they are based on social responsibility and maintaining "face."

This is a topic I address fully in Chapter 2 on history and philosophy in China.

My biggest piece of advice on a cursory level? Don't try to tell jokes in China! They'll fall flat. You'll wind up embarrassed, and your hosts will be deeply offended.

Isn't importing as simple as getting designer knock-offs and selling them on eBay?

There are certainly a lot of people who buy knock-offs online and sell them on eBay and other sites. I can't stop you from trying it, but you have to understand that it's only a matter of time until the people who own the trademark on those products find you and shut you down.

You'll make a little money selling knock-offs, but you won't build a solid business doing it, and you'll be constantly starting over. It's chasing fast cash at the expense of long-term steady earnings in my opinion.

Glossary of Importing Terms

A glossary of importing terms could easily fill an entire volume. Since I get particularly confused with the alphabet soup of international shipping, here are a few more of the acronyms you will see constantly:

ATA – This acronym may stand for either Actual Time of Arrival or Airport-To-Airport.

AWB – An Air Waybill is a bill of lading covering international and domestic flights transporting goods. It is used by the shipper as a receipt to confirm acceptance of the shipment and to indicate assumed responsibility for delivery to the final destination.

B/L - A Bill of Lading constitutes a legal contract between the carrier and the owner of the goods. Typically a bill of lading is associated with sea freight.

C&F – Also known as CFR, this term describes a situation in which the buyer pays the total cost of the goods and their transport from their place of origin to a designated destination instead of paying separately for goods and freight.

CFS - A Container Freight Station is a facility maintained by a carrier where cargo is grouped by parcels for loading on to containers.

Glossary of Importing Terms

CIF - Cost, Insurance, and Freight are included in the shipping quote. Typically used in reference to shipments by sea.

CLP – A Container Load Plan details how goods will be loaded in the container and with what maximum load heights. Details include, but are not limited to shippers, consignees, origin, destination, individual and total weight, markings and measurements.

COC - Carrier Owned Containers means simply that the containers in which cargo is being transported belong to the carrier.

DDC – A carrier assesses a Destination Delivery Charge for the handling of a full container to its designated destination.

DDP – With Delivered Duty Paid the goods are cleared for export by the shipper who also assumes the responsibility for delivering the items to their destination inclusive of all import taxes and duties.

DDU – With Delivered Duty Unpaid goods are cleared for export by the shipper, but the buyer clears the applicable duties when the shipment arrives at its destination.

DST – The term Double Stack Train refers to 40-foot general purpose containers stacked on top of each other.

ETA - Estimated Time of Arrival for the shipment.

Glossary of Importing Terms

ETD - Estimated Time of Departure for the shipment.

FBT – The Full Berth Terms included in the quote cover the loading and discharge costs, which the carrier pays.

FCL – A Full Container Load is an arrangement in which the shipper packs the cargo into a container before it is delivered to the container terminal for actual transport.

FOB – A Free On Board arrangement indicates the seller delivers the shipment free of transportation fees. At the point of delivery, the buyer assumes responsibility for the goods and for the associated risk of damage.

FSP – Carriers offer a Free Storage Period at the delivery site of 3-5 days. If the goods are not picked up within that period, daily storage fees are assessed.

POD - The Port Of Discharge is the point at which the containers are removed from the ship on which they were transported.

POL - The location at which the goods were placed on a ship for transport is referred to as the Port of Loading.

SED – The form required for the exportation of goods is called the Shipper Export Declaration.

SITC – The numeric codes used by the United Nations for the classification of goods for international trade is the Standard International Trade Classification.

SOC – A container used for transport that is owned by the shipper is referred to as a Shipper Owned Container.

WB – The document that shows the origin of goods, describes the shipment, and gives the amount charged for the transport is called the Waybill. It is not a document of title like a bill of lading.

Index

Alibaba, 22

Amazon, 46, 91, 99, 100, 105, 106, 107, 108, 109, 110, 114, 123, 127

apparel, 22, 37, 44, 66

balance sheets, 54

barcode, 110

branding, 98, 112, 123

budget, 41, 101

business cards, 23

business plan, 25, 48, 49, 50, 51, 53, 54, 55, 91, 102

business strategies, 48

buyer demand, 26

buying, 21, 23

Canada, 97, 118

Cantonese, 73

cash flow, 54, 92

cheap, 41, 57

China, 1, 17, 22, 23, 25

Christmas, 42, 112

Communist, 30, 32, 70, 71

Communist Party, 71

competition, 26

competitors, 51, 91, 92

Confucius, 33, 130

consultant, 48, 66, 80, 93, 94, 95, 96

consumable, 43, 96

contaminants, 68

contract manufacturers, 65

Copyright, 123

cost analysis, 26

C-UL, 97

culture, 20, 23, 24, 33, 56, 73, 74, 75, 78, 82, 83, 95, 129, 136

David Wei, 63

demand, 39, 41, 47, 91, 113

earning potential, 26

eBay, 45, 46, 51, 91, 99, 100, 102, 103, 105, 109, 110

Economic Operator Registration and Identification (EORI), 124

entrepreneur, 24, 27, 38

Entry Acceptance Advice, 124

evergreen, 22, 39

executive summary, 50

expenses, 22, 26

Facebook, 78

FCC, 96, 97

financing, 26, 48, 54, 95

Flextronics, 65

Foxconn, 65

freight, 17, 115, 116, 117, 120, 134, 138

Global Sources, 64, 65

Google, 20, 37, 46, 101, 128

government, 19, 69, 70, 71, 72, 86

guanxi, 78, 79, 80, 83

Hon Hai Precision Industry, 65

Hong Kong, 31, 64, 73

Index

imperial government, 30
India, 63
Inquiry Basket, 65
Internet marketer, 36
investment, 26
iOffer, 109
Jabil, 65
Japanese, 32, 77
keyword tool, 36
knock offs, 44
knock-offs, 37, 137
language, 23, 59, 73, 74, 75, 77, 82, 95, 116
Li & Fung, 66
life expectancy, 26, 39
LinkedIn, 78
logo, 99
Malaysia, 73
Mandarin, 73
margin, 41, 52
market price, 21
market research, 46, 62, 91
marketing, 37, 39, 50, 63, 64, 92, 101, 112
marketing strategies, 50
Mast Industries, 66
Minimum order quantity (MOQ), 59
money, 22, 27, 37, 38, 39, 46, 48, 53, 54, 57, 59, 80, 100, 111, 113
negotiating, 23
niche, 22, 25, 26
niches, 44, 100
opium, 31
organizational structure, 48

Orient, 31
overseas, 23
packaging, 87, 99, 110
PayPal, 102
pollution, 67, 69
price, 22, 52, 57, 58, 59, 60, 91, 100, 101, 102, 103, 109, 112, 135
product, 17, 18, 22, 24, 25, 26, 37, 39, 40, 41, 43, 46, 50, 51, 52, 53, 58, 60, 61, 64, 65, 91, 95, 96, 98, 99, 103, 104, 106, 108, 110, 111, 112, 113
profit, 17, 22
profit margin, 40
prospectus, 26
Rakuten, 100, 105
resellers, 26, 110, 111
restock, 43
retail, 22
retail store, 22
risk, 24, 25, 35, 54, 70, 89, 140
Russian, 77
sales, 43, 61, 91, 102, 103, 105, 106, 109, 110, 111, 112, 113
sales portals, 110, 111, 112, 127
samples, 39, 52, 58
saving face, 33
seagull, 77
seaports, 32
seasonal, 42
selling, 21

Index

Shanghai, 31
shipping, 40, 87, 99, 100,
    102, 103, 108, 111, 113,
    114, 116, 117, 119, 122,
    128, 135, 138, 139
shipping costs, 40
Silk Road, 31
Singapore, 63, 73
Single Administration
    Document (SAD), 124
start-up capital, 41
Sun Tzu, 33, 34, 35
supplier, 22, 45, 51, 56, 57,
    58, 60, 61, 62, 63, 64, 84,
    87, 99, 108, 110, 117, 135
supply chain, 52, 55, 65, 92,
    99

tariff, 117, 119, 122, 133,
    134
tea, 31, 77, 81
The Alibaba Group, 63
trademark, 37, 123, 137
U.S. Customs and Border
    Protection, 122
Underwriters Laboratories
    (UL), 96
United Kingdom, 29, 63, 121
United States, 8, 29, 63, 96,
    97, 121, 124, 134
VAT, 125, 126, 134
Verified Rights Owner
    (VERO) program, 123
Waybill, 141
Wikipedia, 70

REMEMBER
Exclusive Free Offer – How to Join

Join other entrepreneurs in our unique **FREE** club –

It's quick and easy to sign up. Connect with others members to share knowledge and experience, ask questions, discover suppliers and make contacts

Here's how in 2 simple steps…

Step 1
Go to http://www.ImportingExpert.com
Enter your name and email address and click 'Join.'

Step 2

Confirm your subscription. As soon as you sign up, we'll send you an email asking you to confirm the details are correct. Just click the link in the email and you'll be joined free.

If you don't receive the email, please check your spam folder and that you used the correct email address.

It's as easy as that.

Made in the USA
Lexington, KY
06 September 2014